Digital Recording, Software, and Plug-Ins

The S.M.A.R.T. guide to

Bill Gibson

THOMSON

COURSE TECHNOLOGY

Professional ■ Technical ■ Reference

The S.M.A.R.T. Guide to Digital Recording, Software, and Plug-Ins
by Bill Gibson

Front cover image of the C100 mixer is courtesy of Solid State Logic. Front cover images of Taye drums, Gibson CL-40 acoustic guitar, and body text photos taken by Bill Gibson except front cover Martin headstock provided by Steve Ramirez.

Publisher and General Manager, Thomson Course Technology PTR: Stacy L. Hiquet
Associate Director of Marketing: Sarah O'Donnell
Marketing Manager: Kristin Eisenzopf
Manager of Editorial Services: Heather Talbot
Executive Editor: Mike Lawson
Senior Editor: Mark Garvey
Marketing Coordinator: Jordan Casey
Thomson Course Technology PTR Editorial Services Coordinator: Elizabeth Furbish
Interior Layout Tech: Bill Gibson
Cover Designer: Stephen Ramirez
DVD Producer: Bill Gibson
Indexer: Sharon Shock
Proofreader: Cathleen D. Snyder

ISBN: 1-59200-696-5
Library of Congress Catalog Card Number: 2005924975
Printed in the United States of America
05 06 07 08 09 BU 10 9 8 7 6 5 4 3 2 1

Thomson Course Technology PTR, a division of Thomson Course Technology
25 Thomson Place
Boston, MA 02210
http://www.courseptr.com

Dedication

This book is dedicated to my mother, Vera. Although you've been gone for many years, I still hear your encouraging words and feel your love.

Acknowledgements

To all the folks who have helped support the development and integrity of these books. Thank you for your continued support and interest in providing great tools for us all to use.

Acoustic Sciences, Inc.
Antares
Gibson Guitars
Mackie
Mike Kay at Ted Brown Music in Tacoma, WA
Monster Cable
Mark of the Unicorn
Primacoustic Studio Acoustics
Radial Engineering
Sabian Cymbals
Shure
Spectrasonics
T.C. Electronic
Taye Drums
Universal Audio
Waves

Cover: Thank you to Spectrasonics, Waves, Universal Audio, Digidesign (Pro Tools), Cakewalk (Sonar), Steinberg (Nuendo), and Mark of the Unicorn (Digital Performer).

About the Author

Bill Gibson, president of Northwest Music and Recording, has spent the last 25 years writing, recording, producing, and teaching music and has become well-known for his production, performance, and teaching skills. As an instructor at Green River College in Auburn, Washington, holding various degrees in composition, arranging, education, and recording, he developed a practical and accessible teaching style which provided the basis for what was to come—more than 20 books and videos for MixBooks/ArtistPro and Thomson Course Technology PTR, along with a dozen online courses for members of ArtistPro.com. Gibson's writings are acclaimed for their straightforward and understandable explanations of recording concepts and applications.

Introduction

This is *The S.M.A.R.T. Guide to Digital Recording, Software, and Plug-Ins*. The title stands for Serious Music and Audio Recording Techniques, and everything contained in this series is designed to help you learn to capture seriously great sound and music. These books are written by a producer/engineer with a degree in composition and arranging, not in electronics. All explanations are straightforward and pragmatic. If you're a regular person who loves music and wants to produce recordings that hold their own in the marketplace, these books are definitely written just for you. If you're a student of the recording process, the explanations contained in these books could be some of the most enlightening and easy to understand that you'll find. In addition, the audio and video examples on the accompanying DVD were produced in a direct and simple manner. Each of these examples delivers content that's rich with meaning, accessible, and very pertinent to the process of learning to record great-sounding audio.

Table of Contents

Chapter 3 - Digital Editing...**113**

Chapter 4 - Broadcast Audio 155

Chapter 5 - Digital Recording Hardware 169

Chapter 6 - Networking Music Computers 187

Chapter 8 - Synchronization 235

Audio and Video Examples

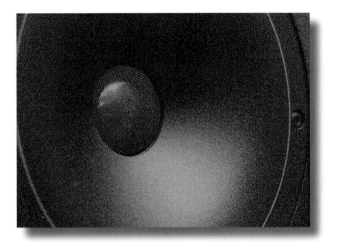

Preface

Welcome to the third book in the *S.M.A.R.T. Guide* series from Thomson Course PTR. This edition is packed with information you need to know about modern digital recording. Find out what you should expect from your recording software, and learn its most important features; see how they can be used to help you produce great audio in the digital era. As the recording industry is constantly changing, our challenge is to stay informed. It's important that we're knowledgable about, and proficient at, new technological advances. At the same time, we must value and embrace vintage equipment and classic technique. No matter whether you're recording voice, instruments, or field audio for a movie soundtrack, you need to understand the digital recording process and the seemingly limitless potential of your software and hardware tools.

The topics covered in this book are very important in music production today. We cover important ingredients in the digital recording process in a way that provides insight on how to make better recordings. We take a close look at audio recording software and hardware and how they can best work together in any creative environment. Also, we see how plug-ins are impacting the way we do music production; we see what they are, how they work, and how we can implement them in our day-to-day creativity.

The explanations and examples in this book will help you, whether you're operating in your home studio or in a professional recording facility. There is so much involved with digital recording and we are in an age where technological advances are commonplace—often, they seem to happen on a daily basis. The information in this book will help you optimize your current setup and will especially help you develop and grow any system into a more productive tool that supports the artistic and creative vision that is yours alone.

It's exciting that our tools are getting better and better. The good news is that almost anyone can develop a system capable of producing hit-quality audio—that's also the bad news. If you're going to have an edge in an increasingly competitive industry like music and audio, you must get both your technical and artistic act together. It's imperative. In the professional music and recording world, we all need to continually increase our skill and knowledge—the process of repeatedly taking what we're capable of to the next level is both mandatory and exhilarating at the same time.

Be sure to listen to and watch the enclosed DVD. The audio examples demonstrate many of the concepts that are explained in the text and accompanying illustrations. The video examples show you specifically how to optimize your recordings in crucial musical situations. Instructionally, they are very powerful. These video clips are produced with your education in mind. You won't find a lot of rapid-motion, highly stylized shots; you will find easy-to-understand instructional video that is edited for optimal instruction and learning.

Audio Examples are indicated like this.

Video Examples are indicated like this.

I'm excited to share this information with you. Most of it is classic digital information that will pertain for some time directly to audio production. However, the exciting part of our industry is that almost any manufacturer might be about to release a technology that's going to change everything! Personally, I can't wait. I've known for sometime that I love the constant opportunity to learn—it is so fundamental to the recording process. If everything was the same as when I started recording, not only would it have gotten a bit technologically boring, but gear would be prohibitively expensive for the entry level recordist, who might be the one about to revolution the creative process. Creativity is always enjoyable. However, the creative freedom that we now realize in the audio industry is amazing!

Have fun! Keep the vision alive!

Principles of Digital Audio

This chapter was written to take some of the mystery out of digital recording. A thorough understanding of the digital recording process is important. Digital technology is very logical, and some insight into the process leads to efficient use and confidence. We'll consider small amounts of information at a time that can be easily understood. By the end of this chapter, you should have a functional knowledge of digital recording; you'll certainly know enough to understand and optimize the process for your application.

Without a basic understanding in this area, you'll constantly be confused and bewildered. Considerations must be addressed in digital recording that are simply not issues in analog recording, and vice versa. Digital recording is amazingly flexible and, as it has matured over the years, has become a brilliant recording process, in many ways unrivaled.

It's important that we first share an understanding of the analog recording process. What we learn about digital recording can best be understood when we reference the analog principles and characteristics.

Let's review some of the fundamentals of sound that were discussed previously in the *S.M.A.R.T. Guide* series.

Analog Recording

Analog recorders utilize a series of transducers, each of which changes one form of energy to another in a continuously variable transfer of energy.

1. An acoustic sound source creates waves in air, much like waves in water. These waves are continuously varying air pressure.

2. The microphone capsule responds to changes in air pressure, riding the air waves like a surfer rides the waves in the ocean; wherever the wave goes, the mic diaphragm goes.

3. As the diaphragm moves, a variance in the flow of electrons is induced, either in a magnetic coil or ribbon, or in a continuously varying capacitor. This variation in the flow of electrons from the microphone is amplified and routed to the record head.

4. The record head responds to the mic signal by converting the electrical signal into a continuously changing magnetic flow. The magnet is simply acting as an electromagnet, fed by the signal that originated at the mic capsule.

5. Changes in magnetic flow are imprinted on the recording tape and stored for playback. In the digital domain, these variations in energy are converted to a binary code representing the energy status at specific moments in time.

6. The playback head is constantly in the state of being magnetized by the tape. The tape induces a continuously varying magnetism in the playback head.

7. The varying magnetic flow from the playback head is converted to an electrical signal that is then sent back to the mixer or to the input of the power amp.

8. A power amplifier boosts the level of the continuously varying signal it receives in order to move a speaker cone back and forth. The movement of the speaker cone should follow the path of the original signal as it was received at the mic capsule in the first place.

9. When the speaker cone moves back and forth, it creates continuously varying changes in the air pressure (waves). If everything goes perfectly, the waves created by the movement of the speaker cone are a precise replica of the waves created by the original sound source as it headed for the microphone.

The explanation above is obviously the condensed version of the analog recording process. There's much more involved but, essentially, those are the key factors. Analog recording has a conceptual edge over digital because it captures a continuously variable change in pressure. There are no discrete steps in the variance in energy levels. Amplitude, electrical flow, flux, and air pressure change in smooth, continuous variation. This system reflects the original waveform in the most accurate way; that's why analog recording continues to be the mixdown media of choice for many.

The problem with analog recording is noise. Even at its best, noise in the analog recording process is louder than noise in the digital domain. Noise reduction and high-quality analog tape have definitely helped in

The Transducer Path

Every recording process, whether digital or analog, passes through a series of transducers, where energy is changed from one form to another. Even without the recording process, the brain thinks (electrical), the vocal chords vibrate to move air (physical), the ear responds to that moving air by converting vibration to electrons that the brain understands (electrical).

Here's a common chain of transducers.

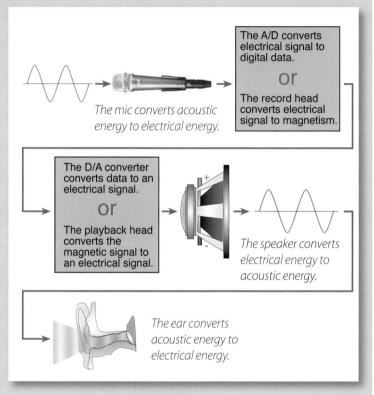

The A/D converts electrical signal to digital data.

or

The record head converts electrical signal to magnetism.

The mic converts acoustic energy to electrical energy.

The D/A converter converts data to an electrical signal.

or

The playback head converts the magnetic signal to an electrical signal.

The speaker converts electrical energy to acoustic energy.

The ear converts acoustic energy to electrical energy.

the quest for an acceptable analog signal-to-noise ratio. Nevertheless, the capabilities and creative options provided by modern digital equipment are just too awesome to bypass.

Analog multitrack recording is a cumbersome process by today's standards. An analog 24-track recorder typically uses 2-inch tape, with SMPTE time code striped on track 24. You really should leave a guard band between SMPTE and a recorded track to avoid adverse track interactions due to cross-talk. Audio signal can mess up the time code track, and time code can leak onto the audio track. Therefore, in effect, you're left with a 22-track recorder.

Analog machines do not have the beautiful and wonderful undo feature common to digital formats. The only way to repair an unacceptable portion of a lead vocal track is to punch in and out at just the right time. If the vocalist does a good take but convinces the engineer to try the punch again, there may be trouble ahead. Once the punch happens it can't be reversed, and the vocalist might not be able to perform a comparable take for a long time. Bummer!

Analog master tapes need to be edited with a razor blade. If you want the highest-quality audio, you cut the master tapes, and there's no undo. Big bummer!

Analog versus Digital

Digital recording is different from analog in that it doesn't operate in a continuous way; it breaks a continuously varying waveform into a sequence of individual amplitude assessments called *samples*. Digital technology attempts to sample the amplitude enough times per second to accurately recreate the analog waveform. The result is a stair-step version of an originally continuous wave.

Since a digital recorder is typically only referencing digital data stored on a hard drive or other digital storage medium, its actions are usually nondestructive and undoable, with complete provision to perform computer functions like cut, copy, and paste. These features make for amazing power and manipulation potential. As we jump into the workings of digital recording, we'll see just how capable this system is of providing creative opportunities for building amazing music.

Even with the power offered by digital manipulation of audio data, musical creativity, emotion, passion, and authenticity are essential. No

Analog Wave Compared to Digital Wave

Digital recording is different from analog in that it doesn't operate in a continuous way; it breaks a continuously varying waveform into a sequence of individual amplitude assessments called samples. Digital technology attempts to sample the amplitude enough times per second to accurately recreate the analog waveform. The result is a stair-step version of an originally continuous wave.

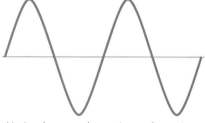

Notice the smooth, continuously varying waveform. This is an analog waveform. To use an analogy to photography, the analog wave form represents reality. The digital waveform, however, represents a grainy picture. The goal in the digital domain is to create a picture with such fine grain that it's not noticed.

At consistent, consecutive intervals the energy status of the analog waveform is sampled to create the digital representation of the continuously varying analog signal. This provides a stair-step picture of reality.

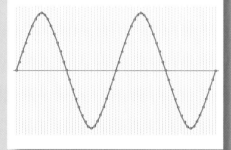

Connecting the sample points creates a stair-step version of the analog waveform. The process of changing the analog wave into a digital representation is referred to as analog-to-digital conversion. Conversely, the process of changing the digital picture back into an analog form is called digital-to-analog conversion.

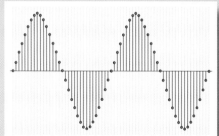

The closer the samples are together, the more accurate the digital version of the waveform. Standard audio compact discs sample at a rate of 44.1 kHz (44,100 times per second). It's suggested that the optimum sample rate might be 192 kHz.

If everything has performed as planned, the digital sample will eventually be converted back into a replica of the original analog wave.

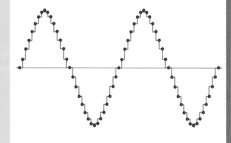

amount of gear can make up for a lack of musical inspiration and talent, but digital tools can help convey the message of a true talent. They propel the creative process, and, if used properly, won't get in the way and slow things down.

Physical Properties of Sound

An understanding of the physical properties of sound provides an excellent foundation for the understanding of the digital interpretation of sound. Our ears respond to an analog wave; our brain interprets the wave by converting the analog signal to a continuously varying flow of electrons within the brain. As sound arrives at the ears, it has physical properties governed by and consistent with laws of physics.

I'd like to review the physical properties of sound, waveform amplitude, frequency, length, harmonics, phase, and speed, particularly as they pertain to your forthcoming study of digital recording.

Amplitude

Amplitude refers to the measure of energy produced by the sound wave in regard to the time axis. A waveform with twice the amplitude creates twice as much energy and has a waveform that's twice as tall. As we delve further into digital recording, we'll see the importance of optimizing the peak amplitude of a sound source.

Amplitude and volume only correlate directly in certain frequency ranges, so it's not accurate to assume that a sound with twice the energy (amplitude) is always twice as loud.

Amplitude

Amplitude refers to the measure of energy produced by the sound wave in regard to the time axis. A waveform with twice the amplitude creates twice as much energy and has a waveform that's twice as tall. Waveform B has twice the amplitude of waveform A.

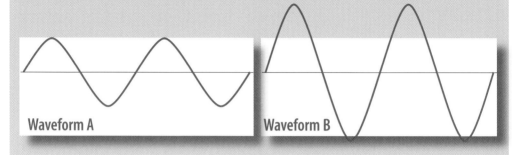

Waveform A   Waveform B

Frequency

Frequency refers to the number of times a waveform completes its 360-degree cycle in one second. The human ear responds to a frequency range of approximately 20 Hz to 20 kHz. The CD digital recording process filters out frequencies above 20 kHz or so to avoid negative aspects of sampling high-frequency waveforms.

Frequency

Frequency refers to the number of times a waveform completes its 360-degree cycle in one second. The human ear responds to a frequency range of approximately 20 Hz to 20 kHz. Each consecutive waveform in this illustration (A, B, C, and D) doubles in frequency.

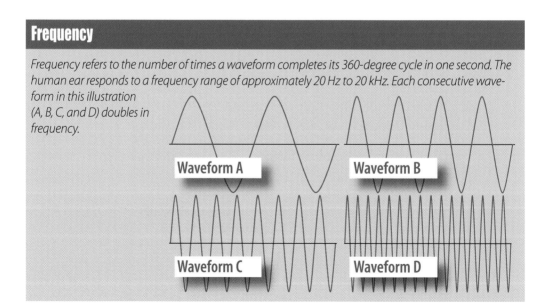

Waveform A   Waveform B

Waveform C   Waveform D

Velocity

Sound travels at the rate of 1130 feet per second at sea level, at about 70 degrees Fahrenheit. This is not a key tidbit for your digital audio study. It's most important in relation to acoustic calculations and predictions.

Wavelength

Each frequency has a different wavelength. A very low-frequency tone could measure 40–50 feet. A very high-frequency tone might only be 1/2-inch long.

Envelope

Part of a sound's character lies in its development and completion over time. The envelope describes this development. A sound's attack, decay, sustain, and release define its *envelope*. Any consideration of digital or analog recording must include assesment of the recording system's accuracy in dealing with the transient attack and the trailing off of the release. A system that can best respond to fast attacks provides the

Wavelength

Each frequency has a different wavelength. This illustration is drawn to scale in order to demonstrate the dramatic difference in wavelength between the lowest and highest notes on the piano. The piano's lowest note has a frequency of 27.5 Hz and a wavelength of about 41 feet! Its highest note has a frequency of 4186.01 Hz and a wavelength of only 3.21 inches.

The length of a given frequency is calculated by dividing the speed of sound (1120 feet per second) by the frequency (in Hz). Wavelength (λ) =Velocity (feet/sec) ÷ Frequency (Hz) or λ = V/f.

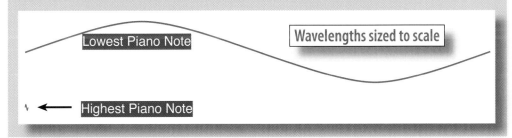

Lowest Piano Note

Wavelengths sized to scale

Highest Piano Note

fundamental potential to reproduce a sound source in a way that is accurate, transparent, and clean.

Harmonic Content

The notes on a grand piano keyboard largely represent the usable pitches in our modern tonal system. They range from low A0 (27.5 Hz) to high C8 (4168.01 Hz). If this was the only pitch range to consider, there would be no reason to require microphones and other gear to accurately reproduce frequencies up to and above 20 kHz.

A *sonic character* is actually created through the combination of the fundamental pitch and its harmonics and overtones. *Harmonics* are calculated as whole-number multiples of the fundamental frequency. Therefore, a musical sound with a fundamental frequency of 3 kHz includes several harmonics, along with the fundamental, blended in the unique proportion that creates its own sonic character. The first few harmonics of a 3-kHz fundamental pitch are 6 kHz, 9 kHz, 12 kHz, 15 kHz, 18 kHz, 21 kHz, and so on (2 x 3 kHz, 3 x 3 kHz, 4 x 3 kHz, etc.).

The fact that the human ear doesn't typically respond to frequencies above 20 kHz does not imply that harmonics and overtones don't exist above 20 kHz. They do exist, and they combine with the fundamental in a way that affects the tonal character we hear. Therefore, it's important for our equipment to capture the broadest frequency range possible to guarantee the most accurate and pristine recordings. A heated discussion brews around the discussion of historical archival techniques. Since we know technology advances more and more rapidly over time, it doesn't take much foresight to see that the techniques of today will seem archaic to tomorrow's generation. Therefore, we need to provide the highest-quality archives possible for the technology of today so that the data will have relevance tomorrow.

Phase

Phase involves the relationship of waveforms in time and the interaction between the waves. Two identical waveforms are in phase when they follow exactly the same path throughout the entire 360-degree wave cycle. Two identical waveforms are out of phase (180 degrees out-of-phase) when the peak of one wave happens at the exact instant that the valley happens on the other.

Digital Theory

It's important to understand the previous information in order to have a frame of reference to help build an understanding of digital recording. The concept of digital recording is actually simple. An energy-level reading is taken a specified number of times per second, then recorded on a grid. The individual readings together represent a building-block version of the analog waveform.

Imagine that several times per second an energy reading (called a *sample*) is taken, measuring the amplitude of an analog sound wave. The first reading measures nine units of amplitude. The second reading measures three units. The third, fourth, fifth, and sixth readings register six, nine, 11, and 10 units. These are followed by four more consecutive readings of 11, nine, six, and nine, then negative values for each of the amplitude measurements. If you were to plot these readings on a graph and draw a line connecting each unit, you'd see the analog waveform represented by this set of discrete amplitude readings.

What's So Good about Digital Recording?

Both analog and digital recording are ideally transparent—they should represent the original sound source faithfully and accurately. Excellent analog recording gear does an amazing job of capturing the depth and

Plotting the Digital Wave

Imagine that several times per second an energy reading (called a sample) is taken, measuring the amplitude of an analog sound wave. The first reading measures nine units of amplitude. The second reading measures three units. The third, fourth, fifth, and sixth readings register six, nine, 11, and 10 units. These are followed by four more consecutive readings of 11, nine, six, and nine, then negative values for each of the amplitude measurements.

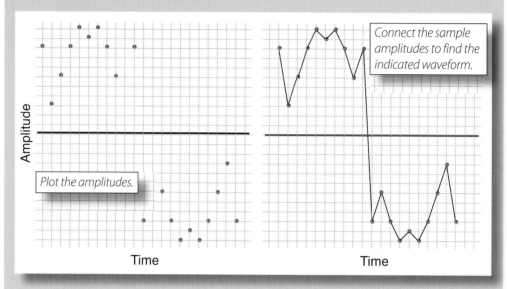

Connect the sample amplitudes to find the indicated waveform.

Plot the amplitudes.

Amplitude

Time

Time

warmth of sound. The fact that the information printed on analog tape is a true representation of the variations in air pressure, called *sound*, lends it an indisputable degree of accuracy. However, constant tape hiss is annoying, even at low levels. High-quality equipment minimizes the noise factor of analog tape. As long as the signal level is strong and the orchestration is active, there's little adverse effect from tape noise. But once the sound and orchestration die down, tape noise is distracting and bothersome.

The process of digital recording itself allows for very little noise, unless it comes from the source. The absence of tape hiss is blissful to anyone who struggled through the analog years. A fade to complete silence is taken for granted in the digital era; in the analog days, a fade to silence meant a fade to tape hiss.

Digital recording offers the potential for a system where the copy is as good as the original—an unlikely possibility in the analog domain. Although there's controversy over the accuracy of the digital clone, the possibility is still a theoretical reality. A clone is an exact, number-for-number copy of the digital data. Clones are more accurate and dependable when the file stays in the hard disk domain. Copies that go to and from DAT recorders and other such devices are subject to an error correction scheme, therefore running a high risk of transferring with several inaccuracies in hard data.

Digital data can be stored on any medium common to computer data storage. A file created on a hard disk recording system can be saved, archived, and played back from several common data storage platforms: magnetic disk, CD, DVD, cartridges, or other optical and magnetic formats. Fast access time is required for playback of digital audio, but the speed requirements for simple digital recordings are met by most data storage systems.

The cost of storage for digital audio is music less expensive than storage of analog audio. A reel of 2-inch tape—commonly used for 24-track analog recording—might hold 16 minutes of music and cost $175. In comparison, an entire album of digital audio can typically be archived on 10 to 15 CDs at a total cost of less than $5.00 or on one or two DVD-Rs for less than $1! Data storage is reliable and accurate. In addition, as technology and storage media change, the data can be easily transferred and copied for future use and long-term archiving.

In the digital domain, the audio becomes data and can be manipulated like any other data. Cut, copy, paste, crossfade, level changes, and undo are common actions. Editing is a dream; the possibilities are boundless.

Digital systems offer an amazing advantage in transport speed. Computer-based systems have no rewind time. Location of musical sections is simple and instantaneous. There is always instant availability of any musical section, track, or instrument. The days of rewinding back and forth through a reel of analog tape are fading. Though many excellent engineers still prefer the sound of analog tape and are willing to withstand its pitfalls, it has become the norm in the upper echelon to track to analog multitrack, then to immediately transfer the audio to a high-definition digital audio format. Working in the disk-based digital domain is far more efficient and hassle-free—as long as your computer doesn't crash.

The increase in microprocessor speed in the '90s made this technology affordable and accessible to everyone with a home computer. Computers are good at taking readings to indicate the status of any energy level at a specific point in time. They're also good at recording that data for future retrieval. In essence, the computer is counting the units of energy (building blocks) at specified time intervals and recording them for a specified duration of time.

Bits/Bytes/Words

A *bit* is an individual integer used as part of a group. In my American Heritage Dictionary, a bit is defined as:

1. A single character of a language having just two characters, as either of the binary digits 0 or 1.

2. A unit of information equivalent to the choice of either of two equally likely alternatives.

3. A unit of information storage capacity, as of memory—a contraction of B(INARY) and (DIG)IT.

A *word* is simply a multidigit binary number made up of bits. The number of bits in a word represents the smallest unit of addressable memory in a microprocessor environment (a computer). The number of bits in a word is called its *word length*.

An 8-bit word is called a *byte*. The term byte comes from the contraction of "by eight," which was derived from the concept of a bit multiplied by eight.

The digit on the lefthand side of the word is called the *most significant bit (MSB)*. The digit on the righthand side of the word is called the *least significant bit (LSB)*.

Advantage of Binary Code

A *binary code* represents the least possible number of digits for the processing environment, where each representation is compiled of a series of ones and zeroes. Anything that's not zero is one. This creates a scenario where there's no question as to the numeric value of a digital code. In digital recording, each value of the sampled waveform is represented by a series of zeroes and ones. Noise on the medium is inconsequential, unlike on analog tape. In the digital domain, noise on the actual medium or a slight hazing of the data has no real effect on the actual waveform represented. If the D/A converter is sent a one in any form, it's registered as a one. If it's sent a lack of one, it's registered as a zero.

With only two possible values, methods for encoding and decoding the data flow are simplified. The most common form of digital encoding is *Pulse Code Modulation (PCM)*, where a one is represented by the existence of the pulse (pulse on) and zero is represented by the lack of a pulse (pulse off). With this simple system and a synchronous clock

Pulse Code Modulation (PCM)

Pulse Code Modulation is a very common means of transmitting digital data. Binary data flow is indicated by a stream of on and off pulses. A pulse indicates the integer one, while the lack of a pulse indicates a zero. This simple means of indicating binary words is common to the digital audio process.

On the sample grid, each of the sample points has a discrete number of possible amplitude steps. These steps are indicated by specific binary numbers, which represent the whole numbers used to quantify the closest amplitude step at each sample period.

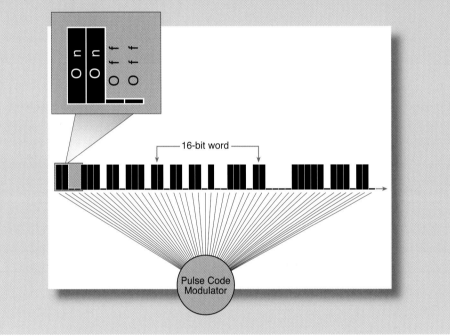

that controls the pulse rate, it's an elementary matter to read, store, and play back the data.

Though noise in the storage medium doesn't register as audible noise, it has the potential to confuse the timing values of data being read (played back). Noise is exhibited as slight changes in the waveform pulse definition, relative to time. "On" pulses are stored as a momentary square waves on magnetic tape or as pits on the surface of an optical medium. The addition of noise doesn't interfere with the processor's recognition of the pulse as a one, but it might make the processor see the pulse slightly earlier or later than was intended. These discrepancies in timing create a phenomenon known as jitter. *Jitter* is simply an audible timing inconsistency, similar in concept to tape flutter in the analog domain. It's eliminated by locking the playback clock to a stable source so that the pulse grid flows at a solid and controlled rate (44.1 kHz for the standard audio CD). All data is forced to fall neatly into this solidly locked sync grid. Therefore, discrepancies in timing caused by noise on the data storage medium are inconsequential. When the flow of data is controlled by an external time reference—time base clock—the flow of data is said to be *phase-locked*. It simply joins and follows as the rate of the word clock pulses with no actual time code reference. Since the clock is a stable source, this procedure provides accurate, predictable, and repeatable results.

Two Common Digital Recording Processes

Pulse Code Modulation (PCM)

Pulse Code Modulation is the most common means of encoding and decoding audio signals. It consists of sampling (quantifying in binary code) analog amplitude at a consistent rate, then on playback, decoding the digital samples to restore amplitude at the same rate.

Digital words, typically consisting of eight, 16, or 24 bits, are used to adequately represent analog amplitude at each sample point. This process, called *quantization*, uses a pulse to represent a one and a non-pulse to represent zero. There are an amazing number of options when using words of eight or more bits.

Each digital sample flows in a linear bitstream, enabling the analog sound wave to be represented as data, encoded, and then decoded for reconstruction of a close resemblance of the original analog wave.

The more bits per word and the faster the sample frequency, the more accurately the sound wave can be recreated from the digital data.

Direct Stream Digital (DSD)

DSD is a theoretically superior system to PCM. It offers accurate frequency response from 0 to 100 kHz with a 120-dB dynamic range. This system encodes the analog sound wave using a 1-bit binary bitstream at a sample rate of 2.8224 MHz.

The Direct Stream Digital (DSD) Process

Super Audio Compact Discs (SACD) do not use the PCM process. They use the Direct Stream Digital (DSD) process, where the digital waveform is represented by continuously varying data density.

In this digital stream:

- *Maximum positive amplitude is represented by a continuous stream of ones.*

- *Maximum negative amplitude is represented by a continuous stream of zeroes.*

- *Zero amplitude is represented by alternating ones and zeroes.*

This illustration demostrates a single 1-kHz sine wave, representing 1 millisecond, in analog and DSD graphic form. As the sound wave amplitude increases, density increases. As the sound wave amplitude decreases, density decreases.

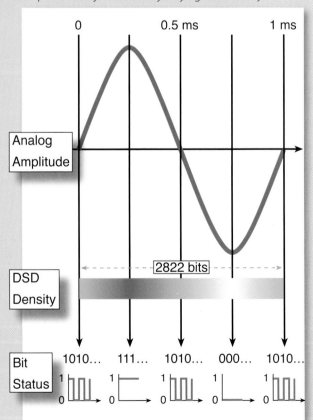

DSD is a Pulse Density Modulation system (PDM). In this system, full positive amplitude is represented by a series of ones. Full negative amplitude is represented by all zeroes, and zero amplitude is represented by alternating ones and zeroes. Increasing positive amplitude results in increasing density of ones, while increasing negative amplitude results in decreased density of ones. With this system and its dramatically increased sample rate of 2.8224 GHz, the analog wave form is very faithfully plotted. In fact, when plotted the varying density looks like an analog imprint with shades of gray varying back and forth from black (full positive amplitude) to white (full negative amplitude).

Compared to PCM systems, which represent amplitude at each sample by 16 or more bits per word, the DSD system represents changing amplitude by the density of one-bit words in relation to the absence of one-bit words.

Samples

The process of sampling (digital encoding and decoding) breaks the time axis (horizontal) and the voltage axis (vertical) into a specific number of discrete steps. At each step along the time axis, a measurement is taken of voltage (amplitude) status. This process, called *sampling*, results in a stair-step picture of the analog waveform.

The number of times per second the processor samples the voltage (amplitude) of the analog waveform is called the *sample rate*. The more times the processor samples the analog status of the waveform, the greater the potential accuracy of the system. According to the Nyquist Theorem—which set out to hypothesize the requirements of a digital recording system in order to accurately portray the reality of a specified bandwidth—the sample rate must be at least twice the highest desired frequency. Therefore, to accurately and faithfully capture a bandwidth

Sampling

At each time interval the amplitude is quantified according to the discrete steps available. The number of amplitude steps available is determined by the word size.

- An 8-bit word allows for 256 discrete steps from amplitude off to peak amplitude.

- A 16-bit word provides 65,536 amplitude units.

- A 24-bit word provides 16,777,216 amplitude units.

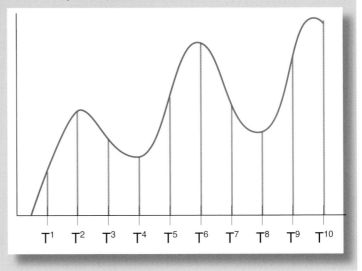

extending up to 20 kHz (the upper range of human hearing), the sample rate must be at least 40 kHz (2 x 20 kHz). In order to ensure accuracy and to provide headroom for the system, the standard audio CD sample rate was fixed at 44.1 kHz.

Controversy follows the question of whether there is a need for higher sample rates and longer word length. Some feel that a sample rate of 44.1 kHz is ample, since filters effectively eliminate any artifacts above 20 kHz, and 20 kHz is the upper limit of mankind's hearing range. Some feel that a 16-bit word provides more than adequate resolution for accurate audio. However, since all frequencies interact acoustically and work together to create a waveform, it seems believable and practical that capturing a broader frequency range and a more accurate resolution is justifiable. We don't yet realize the impact and result of high-frequency content above 20 kHz on the emotional and physical perception of sound. Though the debate continues, many—I think justifiably—contend that, at the very least, we should be archiving important audio material at the highest sample rate and most exact word length that's technologically feasible.

The concern regarding sample rate isn't simply frequency-related. Since no one, not even the newest born baby, can hear above 25 or 26 kHz anyway, the implied ideal sample rate might be 50 to 55 kHz. However, there's more involved in our hearing and perception than frequency. Much of our perception comes from our stereo perception of localization and positioning on a three-dimensional plane. The messages that our brain responds to are based on a triangulation process involving both ears and the sound source. The brain calculates the time delay difference between the arrival of a sound at either ear. As a sound moves around the head, the time and EQ variations are translated into left-right and front-back positioning cues. As the high frequencies are affected by the physical part of the outer ear, called the *pinna*, changes of equalization cue the brain about front-to-back positioning. Perception of left-right positioning is a product of the brain's interpretation of timing differences between the arrival time of a sound at each ear. To complete the system, combined with level changes, the human hearing and localization systems are amazingly complex and efficient.

It has been determined that time delay differences of 15 microseconds between left and right ears are easily discernible by nearly anyone. That's less than the time difference between two samples at 48 kHz (about 20 microseconds). Using a single pulse one microsecond in length as a source, some listeners can perceive time delay differences of as little as five microseconds between left and right. It is therefore indicated that in order to provide a system with exact accuracy concerning imaging and positioning, the individual samples should be less than five microseconds apart. At 96 kHz (a popularly preferred sample rate) there is a 10.417-microsecond space between samples. At a 192-kHz sample rate there is a 5.208-microsecond space between samples. This reasoning suggests

The Ultimate Sample Rate

Sample A represents a 48-kHz sample. The time distance between individual samples at this rate is about 20 microseconds (20 millionths of a second). Since many listeners can perceive time delays of as little as five microseconds between the left and right channels, it seems obvious that a 48-kHz sample rate is incapable of providing the localization accuracy necessary to guarantee perfectly faithful imaging.

Sample B represents a 192-kHz sample. The samples are just over five microseconds apart. The 192-kHz sample offers much greater reliability than other less comprehensive sample rates. Not only does it closely match the perceivable time delay limitation indicated by testing, but it also provides much finer resolution for digital storage and reconstruction of the original analog waveform.

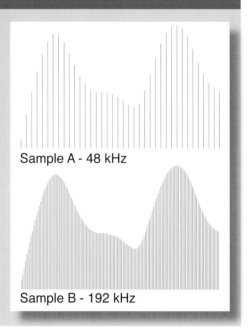

Sample A - 48 kHz

Sample B - 192 kHz

that a sample rate of 192 kHz is probably a good choice. As processors increase in speed and efficiency and as storage capacity expands, high sample rates and long word lengths will become an insignificant concern and we'll be able to focus on the next audio phase—possibly full integration of tactile virtual audio and video imagery.

Quantization/Bits

At each sample point, signal strength (amplitude) is calculated. Amplitude, in an analog domain, is continuously variable. In the digital domain, amplitude is measured against a grid of discrete stair steps. The resolution of the stair steps is determined by the binary word length. An 8-bit word offers 256 discrete levels with which to define the momentary amplitude. The more bits in the word, the finer the resolution.

A word with more bits can more accurately define the amplitude at each sample point.

At first guess, most of us assume that a 16-bit word offers twice the resolution of an 8-bit word: 512 discrete steps. That is definitely not the case. In reality, each additional bit adds a significant amount of resolution because the increase is calculated exponentially, not through simple addition. If we consider a 1-bit word, there are really only two options: digit on (1) or digit off (0). With this in mind, the number two becomes our constant, and the number of bits (n) becomes our exponent, expressed as 2^n—verbally expressed as "two to the nth power." It simply means two times itself n number of times. The number of discrete steps of resolution available to indicate specific amplitude at any given sample point is easily calculated. If you have an n-bit word, where n represents the number of bits, calculate two times itself, n number of times. For example, in an 8-bit word, n = 8, so the resolution is expressed as 2^8, or 2 x 2 x 2 x 2 x 2 x 2 x 2 x 2, or 256.

A 1-bit word is mathematically calculated as two to the first power (2^1). A 2-bit word offers four steps (2^2 or 2 x 2) to calculate amplitude (11, 10, 01, 00). It's easy for us to see all the options when we have small word sizes, but it's also easy to get confused regarding the big picture, so let's continue with our examples. A 3-bit word offers eight steps (2^3 or 2 x 2 x 2) of resolution to calculate sample point amplitude: 000, 001, 010, 011, 111, 110, 100, 101. A 4-bit word provides 16 discrete steps (2^4 or 2 x 2 x 2 x 2). As the bits increase, the resolution dramatically increases. Notice that each additional bit doubles the resolution; that's the power of the binary system. A change from 16 bits to 18 bits is a full four times greater (400 percent) in resolution; if you calculated incorrectly, you might think there was only a 12.5-percent increase in resolution. The number of steps available to define each sample amplitude in a 16-bit word is calculated as 2^{16}, which equals 65,536 steps. In

Bits and Quantization

This illustration highlights the extreme variation in quantization steps available in differing word length systems. Whereas a digital audio recording system using an 8-bit word provides 256 steps with which to represent amplitude, a system based on a 24-bit word length provides an amazing 16,772,216 steps.

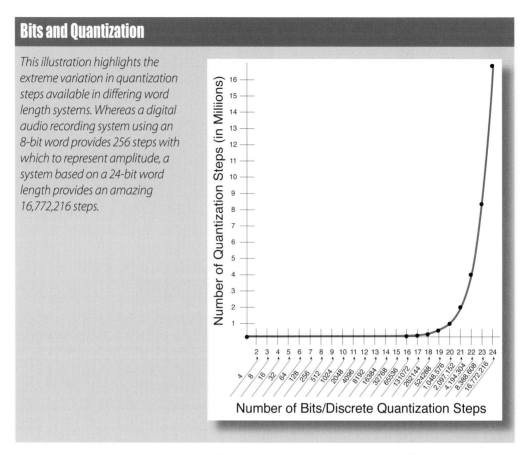

Number of Bits/Discrete Quantization Steps

comparison, a 24-bit word provides a resolution of 16,777,216 steps per sample point!

Aliasing

When a digital recorder attempts to sample a frequency higher than half the sample rate, the sampling process produces inaccurate and randomly inconsistent waveform characteristics. These high frequencies, called *aliasing frequencies*, must be filtered out before they arrive at the A/D converter.

When the audio source bandwidth is properly filtered, using a high-quality low-pass filter, the sample is accurate and clean. When audio source bandwidth is improperly filtered, the resulting sound is inconsistent with probable random artifacts, sometimes in the lower frequencies. Since low-pass filters cut a bandwidth according to a slope rather than a hard and fast frequency cutoff, sample rates for full-bandwidth sound sources are set at about 10 percent higher than twice the highest recorded frequency. This provides processing headroom, assuring the recordist of the best possible sound quality.

Aliasing

When frequencies are too high, the samples lose accuracy. Since changes in the amplitude of very high frequencies can occur within the spaces between sample points, the resulting digital data representation of the original analog waveform becomes random and ambiguous. It's because of this phenomenon, called aliasing, that sample rates are typically set at twice the user's desired highest frequency. Past this frequency, filters (called anti-aliasing filters) are used to ensure that the problem-causing high frequencies are eliminated.

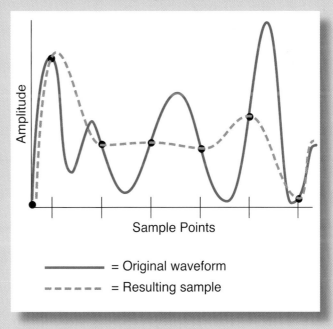

= Original waveform

= Resulting sample

RAM Buffer

Data flow playback rate is important. Since minor distortions, or noise, included in the storage media exhibit the potential to create jitter and other timing anomalies, a system is necessary to stabilize and guarantee accurate and consistent data flow. Digital data, audio in particular, is referenced to a stable, centralized timing clock (word clock) that controls the transmission and conversion of each sample. Samples are played back at a rate controlled by the word clock. In a 16-bit system, the computer progresses through the 16-bit words at the master clock rate. Therefore, data recorded at 48 kHz can be played back in reference

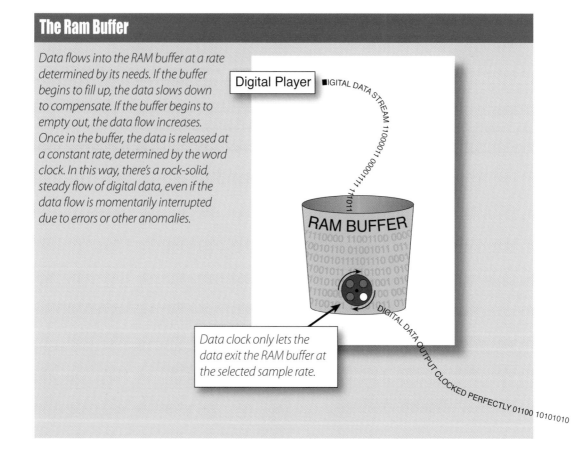

The Ram Buffer

Data flows into the RAM buffer at a rate determined by its needs. If the buffer begins to fill up, the data slows down to compensate. If the buffer begins to empty out, the data flow increases. Once in the buffer, the data is released at a constant rate, determined by the word clock. In this way, there's a rock-solid, steady flow of digital data, even if the data flow is momentarily interrupted due to errors or other anomalies.

Digital Player

DIGITAL DATA STREAM 1100011 00001111 11011

RAM BUFFER

Data clock only lets the data exit the RAM buffer at the selected sample rate.

DIGITAL DATA OUTPUT CLOCKED PERFECTLY 01100 10101010

to a 44.1-kHz clock (or any other word clock speed), but the pitch and speed will adjust relative to the playback sample rate.

As an assurance that the playback rate will remain constant and stable, the processor stores up a certain amount of data as a backup—a buffer. This buffer protects the system from prematurely running out of data. Data flows from the buffer in direct sync with the master timing clock. The tape speed or disc access is determined by the needs of the RAM buffer. If data is emptying out of the RAM buffer, the tape speeds up to fill it in, or the disk picks up the pace to keep up with the data flow. There is no pitch variation, since the RAM buffer outputs the data at an extremely constant rate, which is determined either by the internal word clock, an external sync source, or by the word clock of the master device.

Sample Rates

The number of times a processor samples a waveform is often definable by the user. Nevertheless, standard sample rates apply to specific applications. Most of the following sample rates are common in the digital audio industry.

+   44.1 kHz – The standard sample rate for an audio compact disc is 44,100 times per second (also referred to as 44.1 kHz, or 44.1 k). At this sample rate, it's possible to get an accurate replica of an analog waveform.

+   48 kHz – Another common sample rate is 48 kHz. It was originally held as more of a semiprofessional sample rate until recordists began to see that even the small increase in sample rate from 44.1 k to 48 k made a noticeable difference in the sound quality. Many very high-quality recordings have been mixed to a 48-kHz sample rate, then mastered through an analog process to the digital compact disc format. In fact, 48-kHz sampling quickly became the preferred professional format whenever the project didn't require direct transfer to CD. When developing audio for direct transfer to CD, most engineers prefer to work in the lesser format (44.1 kHz) rather than second-guess the effect of digital format conversion.

- 32 kHz – The broadcast standard is 32 kHz. Most radio broadcasts are operated within the limitations of a 15-kHz bandwidth, so a sample rate of 32 kHz is a perfect fit. The slower sample rate utilizes about 27.44 percent less storage space, letting radio stations put more programming on each medium. Considering radio's limited bandwidth, there would be no practical benefit to broadcasting at 44.1, 48, or even 96 kHz. Any radio show or other program being simultaneously broadcast over air waves and full bandwidth cable could only optimize their sound quality by transmitting at the full-bandwidth frequency du jour.

- 44.056 kHz – This is the original Sony PCM-F1 sample rate.

- 22.050 and 11.125 kHz – These lower-fidelity sample rates are used primarily in computer-specific documents (Macintosh or PC). The primary purpose of this sample rate is limiting file size for use in programming or for data transmission in low baud rate Internet connections.

- 11.125 kHz – This is a low-fidelity sample rate used primarily in computer-specific documents. Like the 22.5-kHz sample rate, the primary purpose in considering this sample rate is limiting file size for use in programming or for data transmission in low baud rate Internet connections.

+ 22.254 and 11.127 kHz – These low-fidelity sample rates are used for playback on older Macintosh computers that don't support 16-bit audio playback.

+ 88.2 kHz – This high-definition sample rate is most applicable when it's known in advance that the source will eventually be converted to a 44.1-kHz sample rate. Since 44.1 kHz is simply half of 88.2 kHz, the resulting sonic quality is truer to the original.

+ 96 kHz – Samples performed at 96 kHz are typically based on a 24-bit word. They provide amazing capability for precise digital interpretation of the broadest-bandwidth audio source. A 16-bit, 44.1-kHz sample provides for 2,890,137,600 possible options (grid points) per second to define the analog waveform. On the other hand, consider that a 96-kHz, 24-bit waveform supplies a grid of 1,610,612,736,000 possible points per second with which to define the wave.

+ 176.4 kHz – This high-definition sample rate sounds great and converts most efficiently down to 44.1 kHz.

+ 192 kHz – Some feel this is the optimum sample rate, primarily because it offers sufficient resolution for precise localization information. This rate converts most efficiently down to 48 kHz.

Listen to the following Audio Examples comparing the sonic character of a few different sample rates. Each example was recorded into its particular format, then rerecorded through the analog outs into a digital editing workstation to capture as much of the personality of each sample rate as possible.

Audio Example 1-1

44.1 kHz

Audio Example 1-2

48 kHz

Audio Example 1-3

32 kHz

Audio Example 1-4

22.050 kHz

Audio Example 1-5

11.025 kHz

Dither/Quantization Error

At especially low signal levels, the digital recording system performs very poorly. In a 16-bit system, a low-level signal, around 10 percent of maximum level, uses just under two bits to record whatever audio signal is present. These low-level signals are common during the fadeout of a commercial song and during classical recordings: symphony, choir, string quarter, etc.

Listen to Audio Examples 1-6 through 1-8 for a demonstration of the digital recording system's efficiency at these low levels.

Audio Example 1-6

8-bit Digital Audio

Audio Example 1-7

6-bit Digital Audio

Audio Example 1-8

3-bit Digital Audio

Dither is simply white noise added to the program source at very low levels (typically half the least significant bit). Though it seems ironic to add noise to an otherwise noiseless system, the inaccuracies and waveform distortions of these low-level signals must be addressed.

Dithering provides a means to more accurate recording at low levels. Noise combines with the signal in a way that increases the overall amplitude, therefore realizing greater accuracy through increased bits. In fact, dither enables the encoding of amplitudes smaller than the LSB.

Dither combines with the outgoing digital signal for linearity of audio playback. Although it uses noise as an active part of the process, dithering is worthwhile considering the improvement it gives us in accuracy and linearity.

Dither is typically selected as a function at the input to the A/D converter or on its output. The correlation between error and signal can be removed through the addition of dither prior to the A/D converter. Therefore, the effects of quantization error are randomized. Dither doesn't simply mask the artifacts; it removes them.

Dithering is typically left for the final stage of production. A recordist should rely on the mastering stage of a project to reap the advantages of dithering.

Noise Shaping

Noise shaping is a part of the dithering process. It helps shift the dither noise into a less audible frequency range to provide the best results with the least audible noise. Digital filters move the dither noise out of the ear's most sensitive frequency range (about 4 kHz) and into a less noticeable range. Noise shaping is not a necessary part of the dithering process, but it helps optimize the process through decreased audible noise.

Dither

Dither is simply white noise added to the program source at very low levels (typically half the least significant bit). Though it seems ironic to add noise to an otherwise noiseless system, the inaccuracies and waveform distortions of these low-level signals must be addressed.

Success is achieved through the combination of the lowest-level bits with specific noise. The noise fuses with low-level digital signal in a way that results in noise blocks rather then stair steps. When these blocks are converted to analog, the result is the average of the level across the time axis. The average closely approximates a smooth waveform. This is far different from what would have been a very inaccurate and grainy-sounding facsimile of the original waveform. Dither, though inducing noise, provides a means to more accurate and pleasing audio at low digital levels.

When converted and averaged over time, the combined dither, low-level bit blocks closely approximate a smoothly rising analog signal.

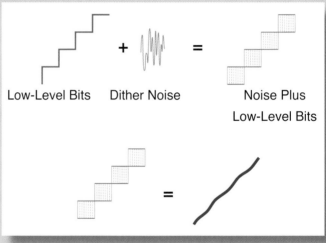

Low-Level Bits   Dither Noise   Noise Plus

Low-Level Bits

Two types of noise shaping commonly occur in the mastering process:

+ First-Order Noise Shaping – White noise is optimized for dithering by including a first-order high-pass response that rolls off at 6 dB per octave below 15 kHz.

+ Second-Order Noise Shaping – White noise is optimized for dithering by including a second-order high-pass response that rolls off at 12 dB per octave below 20 kHz. This scheme also includes a dip in response at 4 kHz, where the ear is most sensitive. The actual amount of noise induced by second-order noise shaping is greater than in first-order shaping. However, second-order shaping results in noise that's less audible.

Converters

Sound originates naturally in an analog manner. The waveform created by any acoustic sound source is analog in that it consists of continuously varying amplitude. The device that calculates the digital equivalent of the analog waveform is called the *digital-to-analog (D/A) converter*. It samples at the proper rate, and it performs all the functions necessary to ensure accurate and dependable transfer of amplitude variations into a continuous binary data flow. The importance of the converter quality is paramount to successful and satisfactory digital recording.

The digital-to-analog (D/A) converter receives the digital data flow at its input and converts the digital information into an analog voltage. Ideally, a signal that starts acoustically and is then converted to digital data will match its analog source once it's converted from data back to acoustic analog voltage.

A/D and D/A conversion is very complex. The conversion process must happen synchronously with the storage medium, the quantization rate must be stable and controlled, and the converter must be capable of accurately handling the bulk of data involved in high-quality digital audio.

The math involved in this conversion is impressive. The speed with which the data must be processed is overwhelming. The accuracy and clarity of digital recording is amazing. Sampling and quantization are performed by the A/D converter. The D/A converter simply plots the quantized samples back into a continuously varying analog form.

Oversampling

The purpose of oversampling is to increase the accuracy of the conversion system. The actual process creates a conversion that allows for a gently sloped and less intrusive anti-aliasing filter. Traditional sample recording and playback call for an extreme "brick wall" filter at the Nyquist Frequency (half the sample rate). A less extreme filter causes less phase error and results in a cleaner, smother digital conversion.

The oversampling process is ingenious, requiring a processor capable of high sample rates. Typical oversample systems operate at between two and 128 times the regular sample rate. As an example, at eight times oversampling, seven artificial samples are created between the actual samples, all at zero level. Now there are eight samples in the place of the original one, increasing the sample rate by a factor of eight. A 44.1-kHz sample rate would therefore be increased to 352.8 kHz. The seven blank (zero-level) samples are interpolated by the processor. In other words, it guesses what their values would be according to the status of the original samples.

Oversampling typically occurs at both ends of the digital data flow. Incoming analog waveforms are oversampled into the A/D converter, providing all the benefits of the oversampling process. For data storage, a circuit called a *decimator* reverts the high sample rate to the Nyquist rate (44.1 kHz in the case of the standard CD). On playback, the digital data is again oversampled by passing through a digital filter called an *interpolator*. This process allows for the best of both worlds, since the data is efficiently and accurately converted, recorded, and played back. In addition, data storage is at the Nyquist rate rather than the increased rate, providing concise storage and premium audio quality.

Oversampling

Graph A exhibits the original sample amplitudes of a digital recording that hasn't been oversampled. The analog waveform is indicated accurately but an extreme filter would be necessary to ensure against aliasing problems.

Graph B exhibits an eight times over-sample of the waveform represented by Graph A. The red sample ampli-tudes (S1, S2, S3, etc.) represent the original samples. The black amplitudes, between the red ones, represent the processor-generated and interpolated oversamples. In oversampling the pro-cessor creates several zero-level samples between the originals. The processor then interpolates (guesses) at what the values of the oversamples should be and adjusts their amplitudes appropri-ately. Interpolation, in the oversampling process, is fairly accurate, especially when the waveforms are free from data errors or other discrepancies.

Digital audio that has been over-sampled is much less prone to aliasing problems. Therefore, anti-aliasing can be designed for a more gentle and natural filtering, while yielding fewer detrimental influences on the final sonic quality.

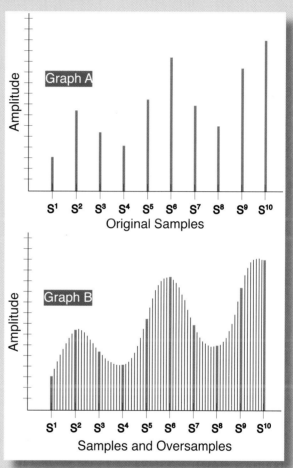

Dynamic Range

The dynamic range of any digital recording system is roughly six times the number of bits. The dynamic range of a 16-bit system is about 96 dB; the dynamic range of a 24-bit system is about 144 dB.

Format Conversion

Digital format conversion is common and involves converting from one sample rate to another as well as between basic languages (S/P DIF, AES/EBU, TDIF, etc.). The simplest conversions utilize unchanged data with variations in ID codes. Complex format conversions relate sample rates and word length in a mathematical manner. Then it's up to the processor to calculate the comparison.

Format conversions can take quite a while to perform because of the bulk of calculated data. A processor converting a 24-bit, 48-kHz sample to a 16-bit, 32-kHz sample must recalculate the sample positions of the new format in relation to the old. Not only does the processor have to calculate the new format data, it also has to interpret the original data and translate it to a form that can then be interpreted. As processor speeds and data transmission rates increase, format conversion will become more accurate and tolerable.

Most conversion software offers different degrees of accuracy in format conversion. In some situations, good sample rate conversion is acceptable: a quick demo, a reference copy, or even an AM radio spot. For music that you've toiled over for countless hours, pouring your complete heart and soul into it, go for the best conversion quality. Keep in mind that the better the conversion quality, the longer the process takes. At the highest quality, conversion of a few songs could take several hours. Processing speed is very important here. If you're doing much serious format conversion at all, buy the fastest computer on the planet. The extra money you spend will be more than made up by the amazing savings in time you'll enjoy.

Errors

It's not practical to expect error-free digital recordings. There's always a chance of imperfections in the media or momentary noise interference with the flow of data. An environment with an ideal signal-to-noise ratio doesn't eliminate the chance of errors. Although it might minimize the chance of errors, it offers no guarantee that they won't happen. Error correction schemes offer a way to overcome error problems, often in a way that restores the data to its original form. However, certain repairs are merely approximations of the original data. These schemes explain the change in audio quality associated with multiple digital copies, especially in sequential digital recording media like DAT.

In the digital domain, two types of data errors occur frequently: bit errors and burst errors. Occasional noise impulses cause bit inaccuracies. These bit errors are more or less audible, depending on where the error occurs within the word. Errors in the least significant bit (LSB) will probably be masked, especially in louder passages. On the other hand, errors in the most significant bit (MSB) can cause a loud and irritating transient click or pop.

Tape dropouts or other media imperfections, such as scratches on a disk, can cause errors in digital data flow called *burst errors*. Burst errors, like bit errors, are potentially devastating to conversion of data to audio, especially considering that they represent larger areas of data confusion.

Data Protection

Given that errors are certain to occur, a system called *interleaving* is commonly used to minimize the risk of losing large amounts of data. Interleaving data is similar in concept to diversifying investments. If you spread your money between several investments, there's little chance you'll lose it all. Similarly, interleaving spreads the digital word out over a non-contiguous section of storage media. That way, if a bit or burst error corrupts data, it probably won't corrupt an entire word or group of words. The damage will only affect part of the word, and the likelihood is great that correction schemes will sufficiently repair any losses.

Interleaving happens at both ends of the digital recording process. From A/D, converter data is interleaved as it stores on the media. Just

Interleaving

The interleaving scheme inputs the samples into a grid in numerical order. Once in the grid, they're then sent out in a way that redistributes the sample order. Whereas the samples enter the grid in rows, they exit the grid in columns. Since sequentially consecutive samples are physically separated during storage, any disk-related errors probably won't catastrophically damage audio quality. It is, however, imperative that the samples are put back into their correct order before playback.

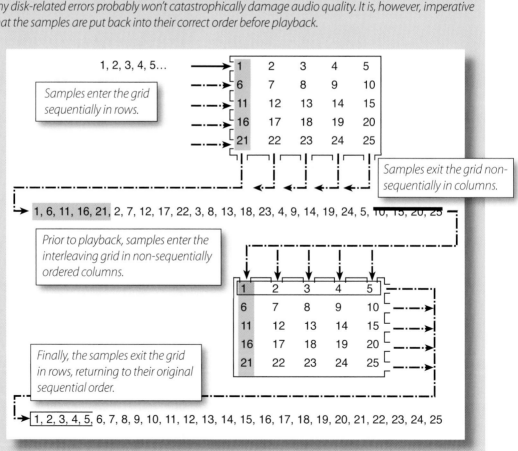

before the data is returned to an analog form, the interleaved data is reconstructed to its original form. This clever scheme provides a system that is completely faithful to the original data, while spreading the risk of damaged or lost data.

Error Detection

Most error correction schemes utilize a form of a code word to indicate the existence of an error and to indicate the possible actions necessary for correction. A code word is made up of additional bits added to each digital word. These bits typically indicate certain traits of the digital word. They're used as a means to verify the integrity of data storage and transfer.

Parity is the most basic form of error detection. The parity system simply adds one bit, called the "parity bit," to each word and attaches a meaning to its status. If there are an even number of ones in a word, the parity bit status is set to one. If there's an odd number of ones in a word, the parity bit is set to zero. Once the parity bits have been set in the record process, they can be checked in the playback process. Parity is checked on each word during conversion to analog. If a bit has been damaged, causing a discrepancy in the relationship between the odd-even status of the word and the parity bit, the word is identified as in error. This is a simple system and introduces an important concept to error detection, though it begins to fail any time any more than one of the bits have been damaged. In addition, it offers no means of identifying which bit has been damaged.

There are more elaborate code word systems based on the principles of parity that are more suited to the complex task of faithfully correcting audio data. They extend the concept to include additional bits in a complex mathematical relationship to create parity words out of blocks of data. Cyclic Redundancy Check Code (CRCC), Reed-Solomon Codes, Hamming Codes, and Convolutional Codes are examples of these.

Parity

The parity system simply adds one bit, called the "parity bit," to each word. If there are an even number of ones in a word, the parity bit status is set to one. If there's an odd number of ones in a word, the parity bit is set to zero. Whereas, the parity bits are set in the record process, they're checked on each word during playback and conversion to analog. For example, if a word has been tagged for even parity (an even number of ones), and then on playback an odd number of ones is detected, the word is recognized to be in error. A word recognized in error will be bypassed.

DATA	Parity Bit	Error Status
1100 0011 0110 0011	1	OK
1100 0011 0110 0011	0	error
0110 0000 1111 0100	0	OK
1010 0100 1000 0001	1	error
0001 0011 0010 0111	0	OK
1100 0011 0110 0011	1	OK

Error Correction

The beauty of the binary system is that data is either correct or incorrect. There's no coloration or subjective influence as there is in the analog domain. If the data is incorrect and it can be identified, there's only one step to correcting it—change the incorrect one to a zero, or vice versa. The trick is finding the error, not correcting it.

There are two basic principles behind error correction: redundancy and concealment. Within these systems, several error correction schemes might be put into action.

Redundancy

True redundancy involves storing the same data in two or more separate areas on the medium, then comparing and reconstructing the data based on those comparisons. If one word contains an error and it can be determined as such, the redundant word or words can be used to verify and restore the data to its original state. The problems with a simple redundancy system lie in the dramatically increased storage capacity and processing speed requirements. Therefore, clever schemes have been developed that add bits to each word to assist in the detection of any questionable data. Though these systems might or might not be successful all the time, they offer partial correction at the very least. Remaining errors can be handled through concealment or muting.

Concealment

If data is lost altogether and cannot be reconstructed through a redundancy system, it can be reconstructed through an educated guess on the part of the processor. If a word is missing or corrupt, this scheme simply looks at the word before and after the error, then calculates the average of the two and places it in the gap. This process of mathematical guesswork is called *interpolation*. Though it doesn't guarantee the exact replacement of the lost data, it typically provides a reasonable facsimile that is inaudible in most cases.

Muting

There is also a protection system in place in case error correction fails. In the case of gross errors, the system simply mutes the particular word or words in question. This is typically an infrequent occurrence and, as such, is inaudible in most cases.

Testing Errors on CD/DVD

It is very important throughout the CD and DVD duplication and replication process that errors are minimized in order to avoid problems. Commercially available, stand-alone devices like the Digital Streams QA-101 provide a simple and accurate means of quantifying errors. Only so many specific errors are acceptable for a large replication project. Replication and duplication facilities typically check the master for errors—if the error rate is too high it is not worth it to process the run because of the increased likelihood of unplayable or unpredictable disks.

CD and DVD Copy Systems

There are two primary methods of making copies of your CD or DVD master: *replication* and *duplication.*

Replication

Replication (also called *manufacturing*) is the process of stamping out a CD or DVD directly from plastic pellets. A glass master is created from your master CD-R, DVD-R, or DLT tape to replicate every CD or DVD identically. This process is typically the most cost effective on larger runs over one or two thousand. It also demands the most time.

One advantage of replication is that, once the glass master has been made, production costs on subsequent runs become much more reasonable. However, on the original replication run, the setup costs must be folded into the complete package.

If the glass master is error free, the replications should be error free unless small dust particles or other debris contaminates the process.

Duplication

Duplication is the process of burning a CD-R or DVD-R just like you can do at home. There are typically large banks of bays that each hold a writable CD or DVD. The copies are generated from the master playback, typically operating anywhere from real-time speed to several times faster than real time.

Duplication is much more cost effective than replication on shorter runs of fewer than a thousand or so copies.

The duplication process is subject to all of the potential error inductions that a normal CD/DVD burner would initiate. Therefore, each duplication is checked for acceptable error content.

Error rates are the single most useful measurement of disc quality, since all serious disc problems will cause increased error rates.

Troubleshooting

The key to success when creating a CD or DVD master lies in the compatibility between the writer and the media. If you are experiencing problems with errors or playability, try using media from a different and well-respected manufacturer.

High-Definition Audio Formats

SACD

SACD, the common abbreviation of Super Audio Compact Disc, was invented by Sony and Philips in an attempt to create a replacement for the standard audio CD. Unlike a CD, an SACD is not stored in PCM format, but rather in a losslessly compressed 1-bit format (or bitstream) that is referred to as *Direct Stream Digital (DSD)*.

DSD is a Pulse Density Modulation system (PDM). In this system, full positive amplitude is represented by a series of ones. Full negative amplitude is represented by all zeroes, and zero amplitude is represented by alternating ones and zeroes. Increasing positive amplitude results in increasing density of ones, while increasing negative amplitude results in decreased density of ones. With this system and its dramatically increased sample rate of 2.8224 GHz, the analog waveform is very faithfully plotted. In fact, when plotted the varying density looks like an analog imprint with varying shades of gray, back and forth from black (full positive amplitude) to white (full negative amplitude).

The encoder uses a negative feedback loop, which splits the output, routing it back to the input—this enables comparison to the incoming signal. If the amplitude has increased, the density of ones increases; if the amplitude has decreased, the density of ones decreases. This system is, on one hand very simple, yet mind-boggling considering that the status is sampled 2.8224 million times per second.

In addition to exceptional sound quality through the DSD system, the SACD format can accommodate more than four times the information of the current CD format. With this extra capacity, a standard Super Audio CD provides space for two-channel stereo data, along with up to six-track multi-channel data, storage capacity for text and images, disc variations, copyright protection, and much more.

A hybrid SACD contains two separate layers. One layer carries the normal CD information and the other contains the high-density SACD information—a multichannel mix and/or stereo mix. A hybrid SACD can be played on any CD-compatible player. However, if played on a standard CD player, only the CD layer will play. The SACD layer can only be played on a SACD player.

Super Bit Mapping Direct Conversion

As we previously discovered, the upper layer of the SACD contains 16-bit, 44.1-kHz material compatible with a typical CD player. This PCM data is down-converted from the SACD 1-bit, 2.8224-GHz process in a way that approximates the sound quality of a 20- to 24-bit PCM recording.

In PCM sample conversion, anomalies occur when trying to re-define the digitally encoded words between mathematically cumbersome sample rates. The actual vertical steps defined by the multi-bit words (quantization) are often ambiguously redefined when they fall in the gaps between samples, which are difficult to define by simple mathematical conversion (whole number multiples). These types of problems result in noticeable sonic degradations.

The DSD sample rate is set at 2.8224 GHz because it is a simple mathematical relation to common PCM data. It is 64 times the CD sample rate of 44.1 kHz; it's 32 times the high-definition sample rate of 88.2 kHz. When five times oversampled, 2.8224 GHz becomes evenly divisible by all of the sample rates in multiples of 48 kHz: 48, 96, 192, and 384 kHz.

Because of the direct mathematical relationship to common PCM sample rates, very accurate conversions from DSD provide an excellent and sonically superior result that is even held as truer than the original CD master encoded through pulse code modulation. The engine that facilitates Super Bit Mapping Direct Conversion, called the SBM Direct, is manufactured by Sony.

DVD-Audio

DVD-Audio takes advantage of the large amount of storage space available on a DVD for the sake of audio quality. Like the standard audio CD, DVD-Audio encodes using pulse code modulation (PCM). The PCM data is either uncompressed or losslessly compressed using Meridian Lossless Packing (MLP), which, unlike Dolby Digital and DTS, preserves the original signal perfectly.

Up to 16 still images per song can be used for documentation, lyrics, navigation, etc.; however, inclusion of video is limited in order to take full advantage of disk space for high-quality audio.

DVD-Audio specification provides for varying sample rate and format definition. Typical DVD-Audio is supplied in 24-bit, 96-kHz resolution (24/96) but the specification allows for lower and higher resolution, depending on the number of channels and the recordist's election at the time of encoding.

DVD-Audio stereo (two-channel) spec provides for sample rates in multiples of 44.1 kHz or 48 kHz, including 44.1, 88.2, 176.4, 48, 96, or 192 kHz.

For multichannel sources, the sample rate is still selected from multiples of 44.1 kHz and 48 kHz, with the exclusion of 192 and 176.4 kHz. Therefore, the specified sample rates are 44.1, 88.2, 48, or 96 kHz.

In addition, the DVD-Audio specification allows for 12-, 16-, 20-, and 24-bit words, as well as Dolby Digital and DTS compression schemes.

DVD-Audio players automatically default to the highest level of DVD specification. Therefore, a DVD-Audio player will only recognize the PCM DVD-Audio tracks on a DVD-Audio disc and will *not* recognize Dolby Digital or DTS audio tracks recorded at the DVD-Video specification. Although these Dolby Digital and DTS tracks are playable on a DVD-Video player, they are invisible to a DVD-Audio player. This applies even if the player supports the DVD-Video specification.

The specification for multichannel DVD-Audio provides for unique variations between tracks.

+   Sample rate and word size can differ between tracks. For example, the front surround speakers might be at 24/96 with the rear speakers at 16/48.

+   If there is no center channel information present, a virtual center can be created based on the content of the L-R speakers.

+   Custom-mixed stereo tracks can be provided by the recordists or downmixing technology, referred to as *System Managed Audio Resource Technique (SMART)*, will automatically render a stereo mix from the multichannel data.

Data Compression for DVD and CD Applications

In many circumstances it is necessary for data to be compressed for storage. Typically, there is simply not enough available space to hold audio or video data at full definition. Therefore, data compression schemes are important—they enable such features as high-definition audio and video as well as multichannel mixes and sound tracks. When data is compressed it is stored in a couple different ways.

1. Lossless, with reference to deleted information for restoration upon decoding

2. Lossy, with unessential data simply stripped away, lost, and never replaced

Lossless Data Compression

Lossless schemes provide a system whereby vacant data is eliminated for encoding, then restored during decoding. These processes don't provide extreme reductions in amounts of data for storage, but they do offer the advantage of complete restoration of the data to its pre-compression state. Obviously, lossless compression is preferable when considering sound quality and faithfulness to the original recording.

DVD-Audio uses a lossless encoding technique developed by the British company, Meridian, which preserves the original signal perfectly. This system, called Meridian Lossless Packing (MLP), is based on the

PCM system used for CDs, although six-channel, 24-bit audio is typical at sample rates of 88.2 or 96 kHz or up to 192 kHz for stereo.

Lossy Data Compression

Lossy schemes evaluate audio, deeming portions of the data stream as unimportant to the overall sound. This automatically selected data is removed from the data pool and never replaced. Depending on audio content and the selection algorithm, these lossy data compression schemes might have little impact on the overall sound quality or they might dramatically decrease fidelity.

Lossy compression is necessary when we're trying to fit 5.1 surround mixes of a complete album onto a CD or even onto a DVD with video content. Dolby Digital and DTS (*Digital Theater System*) are both lossy compression schemes.

Digital Recording, Transmission, and Playback Formats

There are several different standards for transmission of digital audio signals. Each format is, in theory, capable of accurately transferring a binary bit stream. As long as each one and zero is faithfully communicated in its original form, there should be no degradation at all in the signal from one piece of digital equipment to the next. However, if you find yourself in the middle of a room full of experienced audio gurus, you will definitely walk away wondering if any format will ever provide perfect cloning. The validity to each argument for or against AES/EBU, S/P DIF, S/DIF-2, fiber optics, MADI, or any of the proprietary systems lies in the quantification of errors. Cable quality and length also play a role in the accuracy of the digital transfer.

Audio Examples 1-9 through 1-13 compare an original source to three different digital copying formats and a straight analog-to-analog transfer. The example was recorded first to DAT at 44.1 kHz, then transferred though the specified process. Each example was then transferred digitally into a computer for editing in Digidesign's Pro Tools. The Pro Tools files became the source for digital mastering. The only variable in each chain was the digital transfer process in question. Listen carefully to each example and tally your opinion.

1. Original source (acoustic guitar-oriented)
2. AES/EBU
3. S/P DIF
4. Fiber-optics through the ADAT light-pipe
5. Analog out of DAT A to analog in of DAT B

Audio Example 1-9
Original Acoustic Guitar

Audio Example 1-10
AES/EBU

Audio Example 1-11
S/P DIF

Audio Example 1-12
Fiber-Optics/ADAT Light-Pipe

Audio Example 1-13
DAT Analog Output to DAT Analog Input

AES/EBU

This stereo audio protocol is a professional standard for digital audio transmission between various digital devices. This file transfer format was developed jointly by the Audio Engineering Society (AES) and the European Broadcasting Union (EBU). The two-channel digital signal is transferred through a single high-quality mic cable using XLR connectors. This low-impedance transfer system allows for cable runs of up to about 100 meters with minimal degradation, offering accurate transmission over longer cable runs than the other formats.

S/P DIF

The Sony/Philips Digital Interface (S/P DIF) is often available on professional digital equipment, though it's really the standard for digital transmission between consumer devices. The digital transmission process is similar to AES/EBU but is not the same, nor is it cross-compatible. S/P DIF format typically uses RCA phono connectors, allowing accurate transmission over much shorter cables than AES/EBU. S/P DIF protocol provides for digital transmission of start ID and program ID numbers, whereas AES/EBU does not.

SDIF-1

One of the pioneer formats in the digital recording industry was the Sony PCM-F1. It used a conventional video tape recorder to store digital audio information, with both channels of the stereo signal multiplexed onto a single video line. The PCM-F1 used the consumer version of Sony's SDIF (*Sony Digital Interface Format*) protocol. The professional version of the SDIF protocol was used on the Sony PCM-1600 and PCM-1610 converters, typically recording to a 3/4-inch U-Matic professional-format video tape recorder. This combination was the preferred mastering system for years. SDIF and SDIF-1 are the same format. The term SDIF-1 came into use to differentiate the protocol from its successor, SDIF-2.

SDIF-2

Sony's PCM-1630 mastering system updated the SDIF protocol to use separate cables for left and right channels, along with a word clock channel on a third cable, for syncing accurate digital transfers between SDIF-2 systems. SDIF-2 allows for backward compatibility with SDIF-encoded tapes—anything recorded on the older format will play back on the new. This protocol allows for up to 20-bit digital audio. It also includes various control and synchronization bits in each word.

SMDI

The SCSI Musical Digital Interface is used to transfer digital samples between SCSI-equipped samplers and computers. This protocol is up to 300 times faster than a simple MIDI transfer is, and its connections are made with standard SCSI interface cables.

MADI

The MADI (*Multichannel Audio Digital Interface*) protocol defines the professional standard for the transmission of multichannel digital audio. This transmission scheme is compatible with many professional digital recorders and mixers, allowing for the transmission of up to 56 tracks of full-bandwidth digital audio.

DASH

The DASH (*Digital Audio Stationary Head*) format is used in high-quality digital multitracks. Sony and Studer offer reel-to-reel multitrack recorders in two-, 24-, and 48-track versions. The multitracks use 1/2-inch tape with provision for either a 44.1- or a 48-kHz sample rate. These recorders are very expensive and are uncommon in home studios.

Internet

The Internet and the age of information accessibility has changed how most of us function in a radical way. Whether you're a researcher, an e-mailer, surfer, game player, blogger, child, adult, or a grandparent, chances are you spend a fair amount of time roaming the Net. Information becomes addictive, whether you are into aardvarks or Zen.

The future is up for grabs. We see and hear testimony of upgrades and rebuilds and new ways of experiencing this incredible access point to history and the future. From the adoption of a military network to the public Internet and from data transfer rates of 14.4 kilobits per second to millions of bits per second, now we're stuck—something we knew very little about 10 or 15 years ago is woven into society and our lives.

For our purposes in audio, the Internet has changed the way we do business. Simply as an audio and video delivery system, the immediacy of access is a phenomenal boon. I work with a music licensing ageny in L.A. and I live in Seattle. Pre-Internet, if they would call for a specific music for a specific use, it would turn into an event—hustle here, hustle there, overnight mail for 10 or 15 dollars, wait for a response (if the package arrived)…we all know the routine. Today, if they call and I have it, it's in their e-mail within minutes, for free.

If you're serious about your music and recording, the Internet is crucial. If you're not savvy, you must get savvy.

Streaming

Streaming is a very convenient and powerful Internet usage process. Typically, files are downloaded from an Internet Web site onto your hard drive for viewing or listening at a later time—this occupies disk space and takes time. The process of streaming bypasses downloading and gives the user instant access to audio and video information straight off the Internet or network. The data is transmitted and experienced in real time, much like a regular television or radio program.

Many download applications allow the user to view or listen to the program material while the file is being downloaded. In this case you can experience the information immediately while the data is actually downloading onto your storage medium—you get to enjoy the instant gratification of streaming and the ability to access the downloaded files from your computer at your convenience.

Many data streams flow from a file that resides on a server. It's also possible to receive a live stream from a real-time production.

Streaming applications such as Windows Media and QuickTime are free in their basic form and allow anyone with a computer and a current operating system access to seemingly limitless amounts of audio and video information.

CODEC

The term *codec* describes a compression and expansion scheme whereby data is enCODed for compression, then DECoded for playback or implementation. Thus, the term *codec* from COD and DEC. Sending full-resolution audio and video files over the Internet is very time consuming and cumbersome, even at the fastest of connections. Codecs provide a means of compressing the file size to a fraction of the original for transfer over the Net. After the data transfer process is complete, the user simply opens the file and experiences quality close to the original.

Muxing

Muxing is an abbreviated term for multiplexing. *Multiplexing* is the process of combining multiple data channels into a single line of data for storage or transfer over the Internet, air waves, or other data transfer process. At the receiving end, this data is separated (demultiplexed) into its original configuration.

Digital Audio File Formats

Most hard-disk-based recorders import multiple types of digital file formats. If the recorder cannot directly import the format, there is typically a conversion option capable of changing nearly any digital audio file to the type preferred by the device.

Sound Designer and Sound Designer II

These are the native file formats used by Digidesign products such as Pro Tools, Session, and Master List CD.

AIFF–Apple's Audio Interchange File Format

AIFF files are preferred by most Macintosh applications. These files can be used in various software applications, but they're best suited to use in the Macintosh environment.

WAV–Windows Audio File Format

The WAV file format is supported by most Windows software applications and many Macintosh applications, though many applications require format conversion to operate optimally.

WAV files are common in the broadcast industry. When sending source material to a computer-driven radio environment, it's common to save 32-kHz WAV files to CD in an ISO 9660 format. These files can be transferred directly to the broadcast environment with no format conversion.

Be sure to use the proper suffix. In the audio industry, Macintosh users don't need to consider file naming as an important procedure. However, anything entering the Windows environment must have the proper suffix or it simply won't work. (Who thought of this feature anyway?) Always name your WAV file labels with a .WAV extension when they're headed for Windows (e.g., SONG1.WAV).

QuickTime

QuickTime is commonly used in multimedia applications. Developed by Apple, this audio/video format is a common target for storage of content-produced multimedia authoring environments like iMovie, Final Cut Pro, Avid, Adobe Premiere, or Macromedia Director. Quick-Time is compatible with multiple platforms, including Mac and PC. It continues to grow and develop with the demands of multimedia users around the globe.

RealAudio

RealAudio is RealNetworks's format for streaming audio over the Internet. This format allows for various sample and bit rates. Since this is an Internet format, audio quality and accuracy might be sacrificed, depending on the specific application. For example, sometimes an Internet file needs to be quickly downloadable, and audio quality is sacrificed in the interest of file size conservation.

This file format also lets the user determine whether Internet surfers can download the audio file to their computers or to their portable audio file players. On the other hand, they can also prohibit the RealAudio file from downloading altogether.

SND Resource

The Apple sound resource file type is supported by some Mac software applications, but it's also commonly used by the Macintosh operating system for alert sounds and other system-specific audio applications.

WMA

Windows Media Audio (WMA), a codec developed by Microsoft, provides multi-level capabilities, from low-fi audio and video for Internet streaming to high-definition video and full-surround high-definition audio.

Typical WMA audio files (file extension .wma) sound similar to MP3 files and, at a given quality, they take up less disk space.

Microsoft makes Windows Media Audio available for free to willing users, whether on Mac or PC format. Though Microsoft hasn't been a major player in the professional audio world, they have definitely committed to the development and promotion of high-quality video and audio delivery systems as they pertain to network and Internet applications.

Most players support WMA, and online music stores such as Napster and Wal-Mart use secure WMA.

The Moving Picture Experts Group (MPEG)

The Moving Picture Experts Group began in 1988 with 25 industry professionals and has since grown to several hundred experts from a couple hundred countries. These industry experts strive to devise and implement useful tools for use by industry insiders as well as regular users.

To date MPEG has produced:

+   MPEG-1: The standard for storage and retrieval of moving pictures and audio on storage media (approved Nov. 1992).

+   MPEG-2: The standard for digital television (approved Nov. 1994).

+   MPEG-4: The standard for multimedia applications. (Version 1 was approved Oct. 1998; version 2 was approved Dec. 1999.)

+   MPEG-4: Versions 3, 4 and 5.

- MPEG-7: The content representation standard for multimedia information search, filtering, management, and processing (approved July 2001).

- MPEG-21: The multimedia framework.

MP3

MP3 stands for MPEG Audio Layer 3—MPEG stands for Moving Picture Experts Group. It is a lossy codec, meaning the audio quality you encode contains information which simply isn't there after you decode. The actual audio quality is adjustable depending on the user-selected data transfer rate, specified in kilobits per second (kbps).

To simply state that the MP3 codec is a codec doesn't do it justice. Even though it is a lossy system, it provides excellent-sounding audio in a file size about one twelfth as large as a CD audio file in AIFF or WAV form. The acceptance of the MP3 and related codecs has revolutionized the music delivery world. MP3 file transfers over the Internet have enabled the artist to be heard where they might never have been heard and has provided the consumer access to music they might never have experienced. Apple's iTunes along with the iPod provide a means of paying for music over the Internet and downloading to a device that is convenient and inexpensive.

An MP3 file uses typically 3 or 4 MB per song (about a megabyte per stereo minute), which is dramatically faster to download than an AIFF file in excess of 40 MB for the same song. Does it sound as good as a CD audio file? No, but it's really pretty close in many cases.

The key factor in MP3 quality is the bit rate. The higher the bit rate in kilobits per second, the larger the file size and the better the audio quality. In standard MP3 format it is held that mono material is close to CD quality at 128 kbps. Therefore, for decent-quality stereo MP3 audio, a rate of 256 kbps second should be selected.

The compression scheme identifies information that is unnecessary, redundant, or undetectable, eliminating it, or combining it in a way that is sonically minimally invasive. For example, it is held that very high frequencies might not even be discernable by many and that they provide little positioning information. Since two channels take up twice as much space, these high frequencies might be filtered out and summed to mono. The same approach is taken with low frequencies because they are typically omnidirectional anyway. As an audio purist or enthusiast, any of these lossy compression techniques are shocking. Realistically, and keeping all things in perspective, MP3 files offer a great benefit to the musical society at large. Over the years, the Internet will be replaced or updated and file schemes will get more and more clever and efficient. HD audio and video will flow quickly and accurately. It has gotten much better in the past 10 years, and the next 10 will prove to be mind-boggling.

Creating MP3 Files

MP3s are typically converted from existing audio, such as AIFF or WAV files, using software like iTunes, SoundJam, WinAmp, and so on. However, many music production software packages now offer MP3 as an export option.

MP3Pro

MP3Pro is a development from RCA/Thomson that provides better sound quality at the same bit rate as MP3 files. MP3Pro at 64kbps is supposedly the same audio quality as regular MP3 at 128 kbps.

MP4

MP4, the abbreviation of MPEG-4, is another development of the Moving Picture Experts Group. This multimedia format is technically a container format, meaning that it is really just a shell that can hold multiple types of audio and video content. It is streamable and supports many different kinds of multimedia content, such as:

+ Variable framerates
+ Variable bit rates
+ Variable sample rates
+ Multiple audio and video subtitle streams
+ Two- and three-dimensional animated graphics

Creating MP4 Files

MP4 files can be converted from existing audio, such as AIFF or WAV files, using software like iTunes, SoundJam, WinAmp, and so on. Most multimedia production software, such as Final Cut Pro or Adobe Premier, can output audio and video in MP4 format.

MP4 File Extensions

Unlike the MP3, the MP4 file extension (.mp4) takes a different form depending on the type of material contained in the MP4 shell. The extensions include:

+ .mp4: This is the official extension for both audio and video files (and advanced content).

+ .m4a: Introduced by Apple for aac-only files. .m4a can safely be renamed to .mp4.

+ .m4p: This is .mp4 in the form of Digital Rights Management (DRM) protected files sold in iTunes, using the DRM scheme developed by Apple. DRM is a generic term applied to any digital rights management copy protection scheme—not just Apple's.

- .m4e: Renamed .sdp files used by Envivio for streaming.

- .mp4v, .m4v, .cmp, .divx, .xvid: These extensions indicate video-only, raw MPEG-4 video streams not contained inside the MP4 shell.

- .3gp, .3g2: These extension are used by mobile phones.

AAC

The MPEG Advanced Audio Coding (AAC) specification represents an increase in quality and capability over MP3 files. It is also known as *MPEG-2 NBC (Non-Backward-Compatible)*.

AAC accommodates higher sample rates than MP3 (up to 96 kHz compared to 48 kHz for MP3). It also provides accommodation for 48 full bandwidth and 16 low-frequency-enhancement (LFE) audio channels, compared to five full bandwidth and 1 LFE channel in MP3 format. Additionally, MPEG format listening tests indicate that for a stereo source, MP4 files at 96 kbps per mono channel provide increased audio quality when compared with MP3 files at 128 kbps.

This is the preferred file type for music downloaded from Apple's iTunes because it offers high audio quality and compact file size. Like MP3, AAC encoding is user-selectable typically from 16 to 320 kbps. AAC files at 192 kbps approach the quality of CD audio files.

Apple uses a copy-pretection scheme within the AAC format that is specific to songs download from the iTunes store.

Other Playback Formats

AA

Audible Audio (AA) – This is the format used by Audible.com. It's designed for spoken audio content such as audio books and talk radio programs. Many portable music players support AA.

FLAC

Free Lossless Audio Codec – As its name implies, FLAC is a lossless codec, meaning that data is identical after decoding to what it was before encoding—every one and zero is in the same place and in the same order as the original file. Even though FLAC is not a widely used codec, it is popular with the audiophile crowd or any purist who desires sonic quality over convenience and download speed.

OGG

Ogg Vorbis – Developers have been reluctant to implement this codec even though it's free from licensing fees and has the reputation of sounding better than MP3, WMA, or AAC. This is a format that might gain popularity as users grow in their sophistication and expectations for downloaded audio quality.

Data Storage and Playback Media

Once we enter the digital arena, our music, no matter how artistically inspired or created, becomes data. The simple beauty surrounding this concept lies in the inherent ability to store, restore, copy, paste, encode, and decode this data with, theoretically, no degradation. Once a musical piece is transformed into digital data, there's little significance as to its storage format. As long as the medium is capable of reading and writing quickly enough to avoid a data bottleneck, the data should be stored and retrieved accurately. The primary consideration is the data storage protocol. Does the medium use an error correction scheme, or does it simply transfer the binary file bit by bit?

In this era of high-definition audio and video, the primary concern is matching the source material to the storage media. Playback format must match the player and the media must be able to contain the complete program material.

Storage media fall into two basic categories: storage for playback and storage for archival of data. Media like the commercially produced CD are designed for consumer playback on a CD player. However, there are several programs and utilities that provide for audio and video playback from nearly any digital storage device. Conversely, CD/DVD players are not made to interface with your computer for data retrieval or access.

CD–Compact Disc

The standard compact disc holds 650 megabytes of audio, video, or computer data. This medium revolutionized the public perceptions and expectations regarding the audio world. Sound without scratches, pops, clicks, and hiss was easy to get used to. As a storage medium, they offer an inexpensive option to the high-priced portable hard drive formats.

A CD holds 74 minutes of stereo sound at a sample rate of 44.1 kHz with a 16-bit word length.

The CD recording process uses a 4.75-inch reflective disk to store data. The data writer creates tiny bumps on the disk surface in correlation to the binary bits. The read head shines an intense beam of light at the disk surface, perceiving each bump through the change in light reflection caused by the bumps themselves. In the absence of a bump, the light is reflected directly to a sensor. The presence of any bump or pit interrupts that reflection, instantly signaling a change in status of digital data. The concept is simple when you know that the presence or absence of a bump on the disk surface merely indicates a variation between one and zero. What is mind-boggling is the speed at which these changes are recognized.

HD-CD

A high-density compact disc (HD-CD) operates on exactly the same principle as the standard CD—the difference lies in how large and closely grouped the bumps are. An 8x HD-CD has eight times as many bumps in the same amount of space as the standard CD. These bumps are also eight times smaller than the standard CD; therefore, the beam of light required to read the high-density disc must be at least eight times smaller than the standard CD reader.

CD-R and CD-RW—Recordable and Rewriteable Compact Disc

CD-R discs can only be recorded once, but they can be read any number of times. The early versions of this concept were called *WORM* drives *(Write Once-Read Many)*. Rewriteable CDs can be reused just like a floppy disk or a regular hard drive. Though the CD-RW discs cost more than the CD-R discs, they can be cost effective when you know you'll be continually updating data, as is the case with regular data backup.

Like the CD, a CD-R or CD-RW is nonspecific as to the type of data stored on it.

DAT

The digital audio tape recorder (DAT) was an instant hit in the recording community. It was really the first digital recorder to become universally accepted and used in the recording industry. Before DAT, Sony offered the F-1 processor, which required setup in conjunction with a video tape recorder, but it didn't come on with the same fire as DAT.

DAT tapes are small, storing up to two hours of full-bandwidth stereo audio. The transport mechanism offers fast rewind and fast forward speed, and the machines typically allow for multiple sample rates (32, 44.1, and 48 kHz). Keep in mind that the number of minutes available on each tape increases in direct proportion to the decrease in sample rate. Therefore, you can record more minutes of audio on a DAT tape at 32 kHz than you can at 44.1 kHz.

DAT recorders typically operate using 16-bit linear PCM code, though some DAT recorders also use a 24-bit word capable of very fine resolution.

The DAT recording process that has survived is technically called *R-DAT*, for *Rotating-Head Digital Audio Tape Recorder*. This system operates much like a standard video tape recorder. The rotating head helical scan path increases the overall head-to-tape contact speed so that the amount of data required to record high-quality digital audio will fit onto a tape moving at slow speeds.

MiniDisc

This digital format, like CD, holds up to 74 minutes of full-bandwidth stereo audio. Though it accepts the same 16-bit audio source as a CD, it utilizes a data compression scheme called *Adaptive Transform Acoustic Coding (ATRAC)*. This compression architecture essentially eliminates the inaudible part of each word. It relies on the fact that any resultant artifacts or audio inconsistencies will probably be masked by the remaining sound, and that the compressed material might be below the hearing threshold of the human ear.

The audio data is stored in a RAM buffer before it is sent through the D/A converter. This RAM buffer holds up to about 10 seconds of data (about a megabyte). If the player is interrupted by jostling, bumping, or thumping, the flow of the audio out of the buffer won't be interrupted as long as the disruption has ended before the RAM buffer has emptied. Once the disruption ceases, the data simply fills the buffer back up.

Technically, the MiniDisc is a rewriteable optical disc that uses a laser to apply focused heat to encode the binary bit stream. The actual heat from the laser randomizes and rewrites over previously recorded data.

The MiniDisc was originally intended to take over the cassette market and has received much industry support and hype from Sony, its founder. However, it never really caught on and was quickly over-shadowed by the general acceptance of the CD and CD-R formats.

Hard Drive

The typical hard drive is much like a standard CD in that it writes and reads data from a reflective, spinning disk. Unlike a traditional analog tape recorder, the hard drive doesn't have to write data to the disk in a continuous segment. Depending on the condition, capacity, or fullness of the drive, the data for one song might be written to several noncontiguous (noncontinuous) locations on the drive. Since a hard drive's read/write head moves incredibly fast (faster than the eye can see), data can be accessed randomly from any one point to any other on the disk. When the disk spins fast enough and the read/write moves accurately enough, there's rarely a problem with the continuation of the flow of digital data.

DVD

DVD *(Digital Versatile Disc)* is an optical storage medium similar to the compact disc and its variations (CD, CD-ROM, CD-RW). It uses a shorter wavelength that is capable of reading and writing smaller pits on its reflective surface, and it is a two-sided medium that uses multiple layers. The laser can focus on one layer and ignore the other, much the same way the human eye focuses on a close object while blurring out a distant one. The top layer is partially transmissive, so the laser can focus on it or go through it to the bottom layer.

The DVD is the same physical size as a CD (1.2mm thick and 120mm in diameter) and the technologies are similar enough that a DVD player can play back a compact disc.

Whereas the CD holds up to 650 MB of data, the DVD holds up to 17 GB. A single-sided, single-layer DVD holds about 4.7 GB; a double-layer DVD holds almost twice that amount (8.5 GB); a double-sided, single-layer DVD holds 9.4 GB; and a double-sided, double-layer DVD can hold up to 17 GB. The double-layering method is called *Reverse Spiral Dual Layer (RSDL)*.

Video is stored on the DVD in the Moving Picture Expert Group's MPEG-2 format, while home entertainment audio is stored compressed using Dolby's AC-3 standard, which provides for the 5.1-channel surround sound standard.

Depending on compression schemes, one single-sided, single-layer (4.7 GB) DVD has enough room to hold:

+ Two hours and 13 minutes of compressed video at 30 frames per second and 720 x 480 resolution.

+ Three multichannel audio tracks with 5.1 surround on each track.

+ Four text tracks for multilanguage subtitles.

+ Optional flags, placed on specific segments, which let the studios encode the disc to play R-rated, PG-13, G-rated, or uncensored versions of the same movie. This system provides parents the flexibility to assign maximum age ratings to their children's access codes.

The DVD specification supports access rates of 60 KBps to 1.3 MBps. There are five primary forms of the DVD protocol:

+ DVD-ROM is a high-capacity storage medium similar to CD-ROM.

+ DVD-Video is designed specifically to hold motion picture content.

+ DVD-Audio is similar to an audio CD, designed specifically to hold audio.

+ DVD-R permits one-time recordability with multiple read capability. This acts as data storage space, nondiscriminate of format (audio, video, and data).

+ DVD-RAM is erasable and rewriteable and, like DVD-R, is nonspecific as to content.

DVD-R versus DVD+R

DVD-R/RW

DVD-R technology was developed by Pioneer and has the main advantage of compatibility with virtually all players. The DVD-R is older technology and less forward-driven than the newer DVD+R technology.

DVD+R/RW

DVD+R is a newer technology and more frequently offers multilayer media (8.5 GB) and typically offers faster write times the DVD-R. The DVD+R disks won't function on the early first-generaton DVD players or writers. In fact, today's DVD+R media won't even work with first-generation DVD+R burners—they were designed to function properly with DVD+RW media.

Different DVD Media Types

The DVD sizes can be a bit confusing. There are basically four different DVD formats:

+   DVD-5 is also called single-sided, single-layered, and it holds around 4,700,000,000 bytes—that is 4.37 computer GB, where 1 kilobyte is 1024 bytes. This is the most common DVD Media, often called *4.7-GB Media*. DVD+R, DVD+RW, DVD-R, and DVD-RW support this format.

+   DVD-10 is also called double-sided, single-layered, and it holds around 9,400,000,000 bytes—8.75 computer GB. DVD+R, DVD+RW, DVD-R, and DVD-RW support this format.

+   DVD-9 is also called single-sided, dual-layered, and it holds around 8,540,000,000 bytes—that is 7.95 computer GB. DVD+R supports this format. This media is called DVD+R9, DVD+R DL, or *8.5-GB Media*.

+   DVD-18 is also called double-sided, dual-layered, and it holds around 17,080,000,000 bytes—that is 15.9 computer GB. DVD+R supports this format.

Paper Labels; Sharpies; and DVDs, CDs, and Blu-Ray Discs

Paper Labels

There has always been a camp that discourages the use of paper labels on discs. There are two concerns:

1. It's feared that the adhesive will tarnish the foil reflector, which contains the data, possibly ruining the disk. I've never had this happen, but I don't usually use paper labels on long-term storage items. Any adhesive gets weird over time. Labels, duct tape, masking tape, and other such sticky stuff lose their stickiness over time—that's for sure.

2. The label position will be off center, causing the disk to wobble, therefore ruining playback.

Both of these concerns are valid. If you use labels, only use the type that are round and applied by an applicator that positions them perfectly on the disc. Never stick a rectangular label on the disc. The spin of the disc in the writer or player must be even and free of any wobble, or the data will be unreadable. If you run into this problem, peel the label off and clean excess adhesive with something like Goo Gone. Then thoroughly clean and dry the disc, copy the data to a hard drive, and make another disc without the label.

Keep in mind that any potential problem with CD-R media is compounded with the DVD and Blu-ray media because these formats have multiple layers, which are much closer together and close to the writing surface than on CD media.

Labeling with a Pen

Don't do it! The hard point tends to imprint through the thin plastic top into the pitted foil data. You should avoid this because it permanently destroys your data.

Labeling with a Sharpie

It is generally held that it's okay to mark on your discs with a Sharpie. I've done it on a lot of discs and never had a problem, and I've never heard of anyone having a problem. However, when we're dealing with long-term data archival or expensive album or video masters, we must adhere to the strictest standard.

The only problem with a Sharpie is that it is alcohol-based, which could damage the plastic disc material, therefore potentially damaging the foil and the data. TDK, among others, makes a product called the CD Mark pen, which is touted to be free from any materials that can damage the disc or data in any way. A product like this is advised, especially for long-term archival.

Printable Media

It's okay to use a thermal or inkjet printer to print right onto the surface of the medium. The printers are relatively inexpensive these days, and they provide a professional-looking job.

The Foolproof Solution

Don't label your discs. Put them in a box and label the box very well, but don't write on any portion of the disc surface. As two-sided discs become the norm, this is going to have to be the accepted procedure anyway, so now is a good time to start. It's okay to write the date and title in the clear space at the center hub of the disc. There's not much room there, but it's sufficient to indicate enough about the disc to find the box or a database of disc contents. I typically master my projects with Bernie Grundman in Hollywood. He is considered the best at what he does by many, and at least at the top of the A-list by everyone. His clients are the best of the best and he takes great care to have the best gear and to operate at the highest standard in everything that goes through his facility. I've learned a lot by sitting with him over the years, and I've noticed that the last few projects he has mastered for me go to the replicator in a well-labeled box with absolutely no writing or label on the disc.

DLT

Digital Linear Tape (DLT) uses half-inch tape in a cartridge similar to 8mm video tape or Exabyte tape. This tape cartridge, originally developed by Digital Equipment Corporation, became the standard for rendering of DVD video, audio, and interface data for replication. DLT is capable of storing up to 70 gigabytes of data. Besides being a common-use storage program and providing interface material for DVD replication, it is often used for network and automated backup. Once DVD replication facilities developed the capacity to receive DVD masters, the importance of DLT diminished. Though it's still a viable and often preferable storage medium, it is expensive and relatively cumbersome in comparison with DVD-R.

FireWire Drives

FireWire drives, as coined by Apple, i.Link drives, as coined by Sony, and the IEEE 1394 protocol all refer to the same technology. The Institute of Electrical and Electronics Engineers (IEEE) is a professional organization whose activities include the development of communication and network standards. The IEEE 1394a protocol specifies FireWire 400, and IEEE 1394b specifies FireWire 800. FireWire protocol specifies four speeds: FireWire 100, 200, 400, and 800.

Modern FireWire hard drives have had an important impact on audio recording. They are fast, with data transfer speeds of 400 or 800 Mbps; up to 63 devices can be daisy-chained; and they are inexpensive. Digital video cameras typically connect to the computer via FireWire connections, and the IEEE 1394 specification provides ample bandwidth to handle video editing and production as well as very demanding multitrack audio projects.

As computer-based digital audio has overtaken tape-based systems and as file sizes have dramatically increased, it has become very popular for producers and engineers to view FireWire drives like tape. The client simply purchases a FireWire drive for his project. This procedure lets the client retain possession of his own music and provides the flexibility to move from studio to studio depending on the needs of the project. Backups of all files should still be completed on a regular basis, either to DVD-R or another hard drive.

As with any music or video application, faster drives offer more likelihood of efficient and reliable data storage and retrieval. FireWire 400 (400 kbps) drives have been responsible for the FireWire boon and have successfully handled many audio and video projects. FireWire 800 (800 kbps) drives offer greater speed and growth for the future than FireWire 400 drives. If you are using both FireWire 400 and 800 drives, you can take advantage of the 800-kbps data transfer rate if you have two dedicated FireWire buses. However, if your computer only has one FireWire bus (even though it might have multiple FireWire ports), the data transfer speed will be limited to the speed of the slowest drive.

FireWire drives are hot swappable. Simply plug in via FireWire connection, and your computer will recognize the drive without a reboot. When you want to detach the drive, simply inform your OS that you want to disconnect, unplug the device, and you're off and running.

Drives for use in music recording should have the Oxford 911 chip set for FireWire 400 or the Oxford 922 chip set for FireWire 800 drives—either these or better (faster). The big deal about the Oxford 911, 912, and 922 chip sets is speed. Since we know the FireWire 400 handles data at the rate of 400 Mbps and since we know that there are eight bits per byte, we conclude that FireWire 400 drives transfer data at the rate of 50 MB per second. Prior to the Oxford 911 chip set, FireWire drives operated at about 15 MBps, only 30 percent of the drive capabilities. The 911 chips operate at about 42 MBps, 84 percent of the FireWire 400 capability and a threefold increase over the older and slower chip sets. The FireWire 800 operates at 100 MBps, with the 922 chip set capable of a rate of 77 MBps and the 912 set capable of up to 79 MBps. When used in multichannel arrays, the actual data transfer rate approaches or even exceeds the 100 MBps specification.

FireWire IEEE 1394 specifies minimum OS requirements:

- Macintosh requirements: MacOS 9.0.4 and FireWire 2.3 or higher (2.7 recommended)

- PC requirements: Windows 98SE/Me/2000/XP or newer

RAID Arrays

An *array* is simply multiple hard drives working together. The term *RAID array* refers to Redundant Array of Inexpensive Disks. In this setup each drive in the array is striped with time code so that all drives move in synchronous motion at all times.

The theoretical advantage of the disk array is that data is divided equally between the drives, in essence allowing the potential performance to increase by a factor of the number of drives in the array—given an infinite bus speed, this might be the case.

There are two basic types of array setups:

- Level 1, known as a *mirrored array*, sends the same data to each drive. If there is a failure in one drive, another drive takes over and there is no loss of data—the storage is redundant.

- Level 0, known as a *striped array*, divides the data into partitions, or stripes, that are divided equally between drives, hence decreasing the demand on each drive and allowing for more data to flow in the same period of time. The level 0 configuration is technically not a RAID array because there is no redundancy; however, this is a common way to use the array.

A level 1 configuration is not really very practical for most of us in the recording world. If you back up your files with some regularity and have a stable system, the added expense of a RAID array probably isn't worth the cost.

The level 0 configuration holds potential benefit, depending on a couple factors. First is the bus speed on your computer. If your array has a potential data transfer rate of 200 GBps and your computer bus speed is 100 GBps, you're not going to transfer data above 100 GBps. However, for actions like copying large files, the array still dramatically decreases write times. The state of the art for computer bus speed and drive capabilities changes frequently. Before you jump and expect to dramatically increase your drive capabilities by including an array, do your homework—research the bus speed of your CPU and the potential of the array and make sure you'll be able to actually see an increase in performance.

So essentially, arrays hold great potential but only if they're connected to a computer with the bus speed capable of realizing that potential. The downside of a level 0 array is that your data is spread out over multiple drives. If one drive goes bad or loses time reference, all your data is affected. More drives involved could mean an increased likelihood of a failure. The upside of a level 0 array is that you might see an impressive increase in performance and number of tracks that you can simultaneously record and play back.

Blu-Ray Disc

Blu-ray Disc (BD) was developed to serve the needs of high-definition video (HD) as well as data storage. This next-generation optical disc format was jointly developed by the Blu-ray Disc Association (BDA), a group of leading consumer electronics and PC companies (including Apple, Dell, Hitachi, HP, JVC, LG, Mitsubishi, Panasonic, Pioneer, Philips, Samsung, Sharp, Sony, TDK, and Thomson).

A single-layer Blu-ray Disc can hold 25 gigabytes, enough space to record more than two hours of HDTV or more than 13 hours of standard-definition TV. There are also dual-layer versions of the discs that can hold 50 GB.

Other optical disc technologies (DVD, DVD±R, DVD±RW, and DVD-RAM) use a red laser to read and write data. Blu-ray technology uses a blue-violet laser, hence the name Blu-ray. The blue-violet laser has a shorter wavelength than a red laser, which makes it possible to focus the laser spot with even greater precision. This allows data to be packed more tightly and stored in less space, so it's possible to fit more data on the disc even though it's the same size as a CD/DVD. The blue-violet ray has a wavelength of 405 nanometers (nm). The red laser has a wavelength of 650 nm. A nanometer is one-billionth of a meter.

To handle the increased amount of data required for HD, Blu-ray employs a 36-Mbps data transfer rate, which is more than enough to record and play back HDTV while maintaining the original picture quality. In addition, by fully utilizing an optical disc's random accessing features, it's possible to play back video on a disc while simultaneously recording HD video.

Blu-ray technology provides for dual-layer capacity. A single-layer disc can fit 23.3, 25, or 27 GB—a dual-layer disc can fit 46.6, 50, or 54 GB. To ensure format longevity there is also provision in the specification for multiple layers (more than two), allowing for potential storage in excess of 200 GB per disk.

Blu-ray specification supports almost all common audio and video formats and is constantly under development, clearing the way for increases in disc write speed, addition of multiple layers, and other data management and protocol refinements

Data Backup

Be sure to take the time to regularly back up all data files. If you've had a particularly rough day in the studio, that's a great reason to back up all your files—who wants to relive a bad day?

Storage media have become so inexpensive that there's no real excuse not to back up. When I'm in the middle of an intense recording time, I back up at the end of each day. Anything that has been changed is backed up. Sometimes, if a file is so huge that it won't easily fit on the backup format I happen to be using, I'll simply copy the entire file to another place on my hard drive. This is a quick process, and I can simply set it to copy and leave.

In the modern world of recording large drives are inexpensive, and a good DVD drive can save the day. Regular backups can save the day—and the project.

With the availability and reasonable cost of media, as well as external drives, backing up has become much easier than it used to be. If you're recording a lot of tracks, each song could contain multiple gigabytes. Backing up large music files like these to CD has become impractical, especially if you're talking about an entire album of 10 or 12 songs. My final album backups are between 25 and 60 GB, and even considering the full 750-MB storage space per CD, that works out to 40 to 60 CDs to back up an album! DVD-R media came to the rescue with 4.7 GB of storage per layer. Considering DVD-R specification provides for dual-layer, two-sided media, the DVD potential is almost 19 GB—that's more like it. And now with the advent of Blu-ray disks, which store an impressive 25 GB per layer, there is a realistic storage and archival media. Blu-ray specification provides for multiple-layer, two-sided media that holds a potential 200+ GB—that should be enough to hold a complete project for the foreseeable future.

The Problem with Backing Up to CD-R, DVD-R, or Blu-Ray

There are two main issues with backing up to writeable and rewritable media such as CD, DVD, and Blu-ray.

Speed

Even at 8X, 16X, or 32X write speeds, larger files take a long time to back up. The file must be written and then it must be verified; this process has gotten more tolerable as the write times have gotten faster, but if you own a drive that writes at 1X only, backing up a full-scale album could be a day-long event.

Durability/Longevity

It still remains to be seen how these discs will withstand the test of time. We've really only had CD-R available for a relatively brief moment in audio history, yet we're starting to see signs that CD-R and DVD-R media start to deteriorate when stored for long periods of time. To minimize problems, buy media manufactured by well-respected companies. Kodak has a good reputation, as do TDK, Taiyo Yuden, and others. Here is where you need to research the product of the day. I could tell what the media of today is, but that might change tomorrow. Do yourself a favor and go see the most well-respected audio dealers in your area—ask them what the media of the day is. If they're good, they'll have an intelligent and valuable answer. Develop a relationship with them and buy gear from them. In this day of mail order and the Internet, we often sell relationships short in the music business. There are two business relationships you should have in life: your banker and your pro audio dealer.

Backing Up to Auxiliary Hard Drives

Drives have gotten less expensive and they're much faster than any writeable disk like CD-R, DVD-R, or Blu-ray. I've found that considering an external FireWire drive as media cost to the client is very efficient and easily justifiable. I'll either record the project to one of my drives and back up to theirs on a regular basis or simply record to the client drive and back up to DVD-R. This way the client pays for the drive, you don't need to buy 10 drives, and the client feels more ownership in the project.

Backup Utilities

Whenever you're backing up large amounts of data, some kind of software-based backup utility is essential. This valuable software should help at the very least with three crucial tasks.

1. Spreading large amounts of data out over several discs. A backup utility lets you drag a group of files onto a list, and then if your data occupies multiple discs, the software divides the data between the discs. Without this tool, you need to choose just enough data to fill up a disc, and you must divide files manually or waste a lot of disc space. This is all very cumbersome and time consuming. It's

much nicer if the utility performs these takes and it's also much easier to restore later.

2. Automatically backing up data on a regular schedule. If you're anything like the rest of the human population, you get busy and little details, like backing up your music files, get lost in the shuffle. Backup software comes to the rescue. Simply schedule backups. You choose the source and the destination for each file on your backup list. This process works best for regular backups to auxiliary drives. If you designate a hard drive other than the drive your music project is on as the target for your backups and schedule a daily backup, you'll always be safe. Schedule the backup time for the middle of the night or sometime when you're least active on your computer.

3. Keeping track of and restoring archived data. Once data has been spread out across multiple discs, it's not always that easy to put back together. Your backup software should automate this process, at the very least asking for each disc required to restore your project. When backing up data, you will be prompted for the title of each disc. I always write the title on the disc along with the disc number and the number of discs in the archive.

Conclusion

It's really quite amazing how far technology has come in the past 10 years, and it seems like every month brings something new to the playing field. If you're serious about your craft, keep up on what's new and do your best to implement it into your routine as quickly as humanly and financially possible. At the same time, don't lose sight of the value of your current and vintage gear. These are all just tools to have in your toolbox, arrows to have in your quiver, straws to have in your shake. Anyway, have fun!

Audio Recording Software

Things to Look for in the Software You Choose

It's in the best interest of the user to select software from a company that has made proactive strides forward in the industry. Industry leaders tend to survive; trend followers don't. There's nothing more frustrating than buying high-priced software, only to see the manufacturer go out of business a year or so later. Technical support is lost, the possibility of upgraded or improved functionality is gone, and new software must be purchased in order to keep competitive and current.

Check into technical support. The reputation of the tech support staff is easy to discover. Go to the online user group Web site for the manufacturers you're considering. Eavesdrop on the conversation. Pay attention to the tone of the participants. If they're angrily complaining about the lack of technical support or about the incredible difficulty getting through on the telephone lines, be careful. Any popular product inspires a plethora of tech support calls, so be patient, but also be assertive. If the manufacturers are selling massive quantities of their wares, they probably should be able to afford adequate support.

If possible, get a demo version of each software package you're considering. Most companies have demo versions of their wares available on their Web site, or they'll usually be happy to send a demo copy for review. The demo versions are usually disabled in some way, but they provide a good test drive. If you open the software and everything makes sense, that's a good sign. If you open the software and you struggle to get anything to happen, that's a bad sign. Many packages are difficult to use at first. Then, once you learn a few basic procedures, everything falls into place. However, there's positive value in a program that's user-friendly, a program with which you can effortlessly perform basic functions.

Differences between Hard Disk and Tape-Based Recording

Linear versus Nonlinear

Tape recorders are a linear, sequential medium. You need to fast forward or rewind the tape in order to hear or record at a specific time point. Whether using a reel-to-reel machine or a modular digital multitrack, the time it takes for the tape to physically wind to the correct spot can be detrimental to the flow of a session.

Hard disk recording is, however, a nonlinear—also called *random access*—medium. Any point in the timeline of your recording is instantly accessible. A keystroke or mouse click immediately locates and plays from any point in your recording. This kind of immediacy becomes an integral part of the recording process. The ability to locate a specified point to perform or repeat a take enables everyone to maintain focus—to get the job done most effectively. Given too much lag time, someone is bound to crack a joke or get hungry, thirsty, cranky, or just goofy.

Destructive versus Nondestructive Editing

Whereas a punch-in on a tape-based system obliterates whatever was previously on the tape, hard disk systems allow for completely nondestructive recording and editing. There's no need to erase any take or track, as long as there's enough hard disk space remaining. The nondestructive nature of hard disk-based digital recording systems provides an environment that is much less stressful and much more productive and efficient than that of tape-based recording.

Number of Tracks and Takes

Tape has a limited number of tracks. Once the tracks are full, something needs to be erased before something else is recorded. If you are pretty sure you've gotten the hottest guitar solo but the guitarist wants to give it just one more try, you need to quickly evaluate, commit, and destroy what could be the only good take of the day.

In the hard disk arena, takes and tracks aren't necessarily the same thing. Most high-end software packages provide for multiple takes on any given track; each take is kept unless you really want to erase it. The only limitation is hard disk space. I typically record 10 to 20 lead vocal takes that end up fitting together during mixdown, but those 10 to 20 takes only represent options on one track. Try that on a tape-based system! If four vocalists are recorded, each with 10 to 20 takes, along with a full band and several instrumental solo takes, imagine the massive number of tracks that could quickly be used up.

Terms Common to Hard Disk Recording

Some terminology used in hard disk recording is slightly different from the common terminology in the analog domain. These terms often describe a completely new way to work. Sometimes, they use the familiar imagery of terms common to the analog era—possibly with a slightly different application.

Track

A *track* in a digital-audio software package is similar to a track in a MIDI software package. Whereas the MIDI track contains MIDI data, the audio track refers to digital audio that's located on the hard drive. Tracks in both these applications are different from the traditional use of the term in the multitrack domain. Tracks on an analog reel-to-reel, MDM, or cassette multitrack are finite in number—if the machine is an eight-track, there are eight tracks. Software-based systems allow for relatively unlimited numbers of tracks. Typically, the number of tracks is only limited by the amount of available hard disk space.

Voice

Voices are closely related to tracks, but they're limited in their availability. Voices define the possible number of active digital tracks. A system that allows for eight voices can only have eight tracks playing at once. Each track must be assigned to a voice to be heard. Multiple tracks can't play on the same voice at the same time. However, tracks can share a voice if they don't play at the same time.

Take

A *take* is an optional variation of a track. The number of takes is typically limited only by the amount of available hard disk space. Once the lead vocal track has been recorded, for example, another version of the lead vocal can be recorded without creating a new lead vocal track. By simply selecting a new take, the track can be recorded again as an additional take. Though the concept of takes is similar to simply adding additional tracks, they offer a much more organized approach to digital multitrack recording. Only so much fits on the computer monitor, no matter how large it is. Takes let the user keep the conceptual number

Voices

A digital recording system typically offers a limited number of playback voices. The number of available voices is usually variable, depending on the processor power and available RAM.

The screen below contains an eight-voice system, meaning eight simultaneous audio tracks can be played back at once—the two lead vocal tracks and all the BGVs can play back at once.

Notice the Lead Vocal 1 track and the Bass Guitar track occupy the same voice and are simultaneously active. In this scenario, only the Lead Vocal 1 track would play back. The bass guitar wouldn't be heard at all until the lead vocal track became empty. A feature called dynamic allocation distributes multiple audio tracks to play back from a common voice. Typically, the track highest up on the track list is allocated the voice first. The rest must wait for the voice to become available.

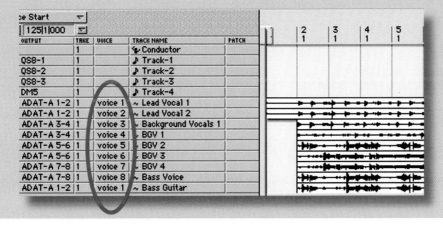

of tracks to a minimum while still providing a system to store options. If you created a new track for each new take, you'd soon find yourself in the middle an organizational nightmare. Using takes helps keep your files easy to manage, follow, and understand.

Channel

A *channel* is a mixer feature. In the MDM, reel-to-reel, and cassette multitrack domains, tracks always refer to machine capacity and channels refer to mixer capacity. There are no tracks on a mixer and there are no channels on a machine. In the software domain, channels still refer to mixer capacity, whether hardware- or software-based. Each track within a software system can have a mixer channel.

Takes

Takes provide a means of recording alternate versions of any track without creating an unmanageable mass of tracks. Multiple takes are accessed easily though the Takes pop-up list. Simply select the desired take and you're right where you want to be. This feature is very useful when recording multiple takes of a vocal or solo track. Keep adding takes, then later go back through each take to find the best portions to combine for the final version.

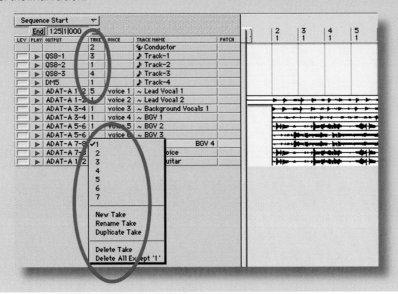

However, the audio from the track won't be heard unless there's a voice available for playback.

Crossfade

The *crossfade* is commonly used to feather regions together—while one region turns down, the other region turns up. They blend in a way that's inconspicuous and sonically smooth. Crossfades typically provide the answer to an awkward edit scenario.

Audio Engine

The *audio engine* is the software that defines the handling of digital audio within the computer domain. Most manufacturers optimize their products for use with their own audio engine. Many manufacturers cooperate in a way that's beneficial to the consumer. Since most software packages are primarily a user interface created to facilitate manipulation of a combined audio and MIDI environment, manufacturers are less proprietary about the specific engine used to handle audio needs. Some packages provide multiple audio engine selections, chosen directly from the software-driven menus.

DSP

DSP stands for *digital signal processor*. The DSP is responsible for the manipulation of digital audio data. Effects, equalization,

Channels

Channels are a mixer feature. Whereas tracks refer to machine capacity, channels refer to mixer capacity. There are no tracks on a mixer and there are no channels on a machine. In the software domain, channels still refer to mixer capacity, whether hardware- or software-based. Each track within a software system can have a mixer channel. However, the audio from the track won't be heard unless there's a voice available for playback.

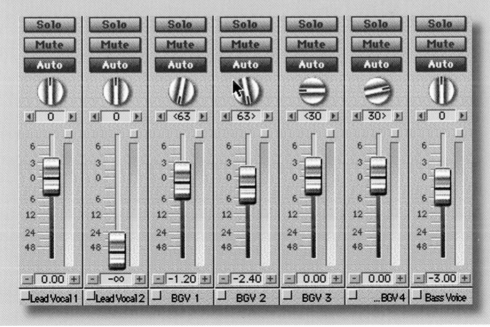

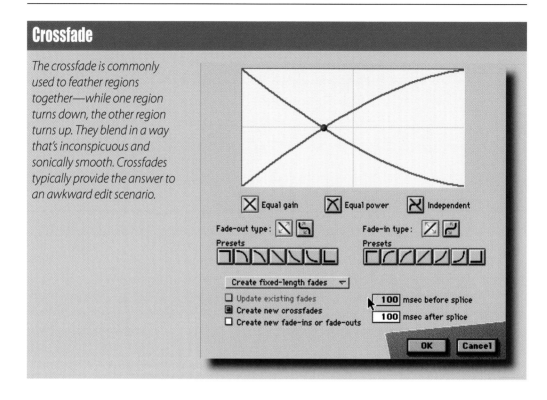

Crossfade

The crossfade is commonly used to feather regions together—while one region turns down, the other region turns up. They blend in a way that's inconspicuous and sonically smooth. Crossfades typically provide the answer to an awkward edit scenario.

normalization, time compression and expansion, dynamics, and so on are all performed through digital signal processing. In a computer-based system, the DSP functions are handled by the same processor that runs the computer, unless there is a sound card containing additional DSP. The more DSP that's available, the less drain that is placed on the system. Digidesign offers a special audio card called the *DSP farm* that contains several DSP chips. A card like this lets the user apply multiple plug-ins and effects in a mixing and playback setting without overtaxing the computer. When there's not enough DSP available, problems start to crop up. Effects either don't work or only work part of the time, systems crash, tracks might disappear, settings might disappear, or the entire system might slow way down. It's obviously better to have enough DSP available to do the job right.

Pre-Roll

Pre-roll is a term borrowed from the video editing field. When a transport automatically rewinds for playback, the amount of time it rewinds before the actual locate point is called the pre-roll. Pre-roll is used to get a running start at the locate point, which is typically an edit point of some type. In the mechanical transport domain, pre-roll is used to allow time for all machines to synchronize so the edit point can be accurately assessed. In the digital audio domain, the same considerations might be a factor if mechanical transports are locking to the digital platform. If there are no mechanical transports, pre-roll simply provides ramp-up time for the brain to accurately understand what it's hearing.

Post-Roll

Post-roll is the amount of time the mechanical or digital transport plays after the locate point. Post-roll is used to let the user hear the edit/locate point in context.

Dedicated Proprietary Systems

There are several systems on the market that contain the mixer, the processor, the hard drives, and the proprietary operating system all in one box. Roland, Boss, and Korg have done a good job of housing some very powerful recording features in the systems, including many editing features, effects, and mix automation, to name just a few.

The Upside

Sonically, these systems do a good job. It depends on the device whether you can record high-definition audio, but typically these tools are used for song demos and small-scale projects that don't need to be recorded in HD. They offer great features like effects, moving faders, good EQ, well-thought-out operating systems, and compact size.

These systems are excellent tools for songwriting and small demos. You typically have 16 or 32 tracks of audio to work with, as well as some MIDI features. They're convenient to use and you can walk out of the store with everything you need to record your music, all in one box, ready to go. Just add a microphone and some creative magic, and you're in the game.

The Downside

Once you purchase these all-in-one systems, you're locked into that piece of hardware until you decide to move on. Even with OS updates, you're still stuck with the same small screen to search the maze of commands with, the same basic features, and similar functionality. These systems just don't provide much room for growth. Even though some systems provide for syncing multiple recorders, you still get nowhere near the flexibility and upgradability offered by a software-based system and a powerful CPU.

Personal Computer-Based Recording Systems

Computer-based recording systems are the workhorses of the audio industry. There are several excellent software packages that provide powerful, professional features that let the user perform world-class tasks, whether at home or in a world-class studio. With the growth of plug-ins and the increased power of the computer processor, it seems that the possibilities for creative bliss are limitless.

These systems are all about the software you choose. The beauty of the software industry is its competitive nature. From the birth of the computer-based MIDI sequencer through today's integrated MIDI/audio recording packages, the battle of one-upsmanship and technological leapfrog is in full force. We, the consumers, win! The price drops and the features become nearly identical.

The Upside

The upside of these systems is power and longevity. When the software changes, you often get what feels like a brand-new and way cooler system. Features that you're dreaming of and waiting for show up. All you have to do is install the new software. Also, you get to grow with the system; every time an upgrade comes out, you simply add a few more tricks to your bag and your depth with the system increases. Before you know it, you're pretty good with your software.

In addition, if you need more processing power, with this type of system you simply upgrade your current computer or you buy a brand new hot rod of a CPU.

These systems often require hardware interfaces for digital audio and timing and MIDI control. Though this adds a cost factor, it also adds an amazing amount of power and flexibility. If you want to upgrade from a CD-quality 44.1/16 system to HD audio, all you need to do is replace the audio interface with an HD-capable piece of hardware. Your system still feels and looks the same, but your audio quality has dramatically increased, and you only had to invest in one piece of hardware rather than in an entirely new system.

The Downside

You must decide what your goal is with your system. If you're not particularly technically inclined and if you just want to record song demos, a computer-based system might be a little too much to start with. If you start with the all-in-one system you'll most likely eventually end up with a computer-based system, but you will have been able to learn the fundamental principles in a simpler and less sophisticated setting.

There is usually much more to putting together a system than the first-time buyer realizes, especially with a software-based studio. You will probably need to get a mixer, an audio interface, a MIDI interface, some mics, all the right cables, and enough AC access to plug everything in. Then you'll need to get everything working together. This is a simple task for someone who knows what he or she is doing, but if you're new to digital recording systems, you might just end up frustrated and confused.

Comparison of Component and All-in-One Recording Systems

Recording systems comprised of multiple components are complex and powerful and they typically sound good. The all-in-one portable studio is simple and streamlined but might sacrifice sound quality. The illustration below provides a graphic example of the increased complexity of the component system.

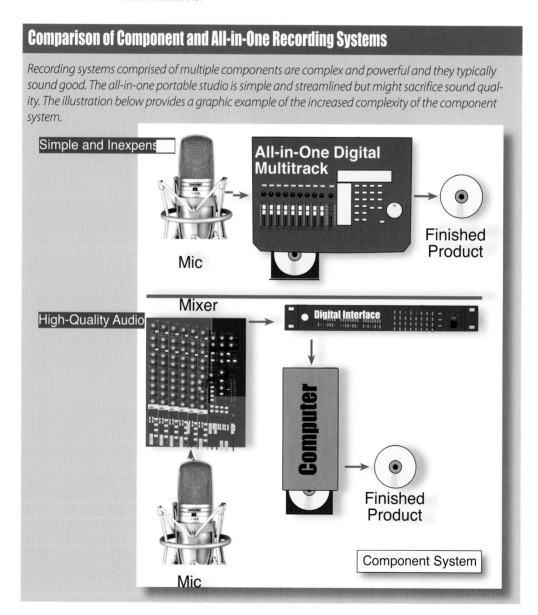

I am a big fan of the software-based computer-centered studio but you must realize what you're getting into if you're new, and you must be willing to focus and learn a lot of stuff quickly.

The Classics in Audio Recording Software Packages

There are excellent software packages manufactured by Digidesign, Mark of the Unicorn, Steinberg, Apple, Cakewalk, and many more. There is little value in creating long list of each program that's available today, because you really need the status of the industry on the day you read this book. I can, however, provide a list of some of the industry mainstays, along with a list of features and functions you should look for and expect in your software.

These digital audio recording software packages represent the manufacturers who have had long-term impact on the recording industry. They all provide excellent features and they have all been around long enough to offer very stable and well-tested platforms. Countless hits have been recorded on each platform; they are professional products, used by professionals; and they continually strive to provide competitive packages. When one manufacturer makes a breakthough with a new creative tool, the others typically incorporate the same tool soon thereafter. Each of these companies has made advances that the others have had to mimic—they all try hard and they all provide professional, feature-laden, forward-thinking software.

Pro Tools by Digidesign (Windows and Mac)

Digidesign has created a product and a marketing scheme that has dominated the high-end professional studio world. As a rule, their software, hardware, and plug-ins are the most expensive in the industry—there might be certain exceptions, but not many. However, they have continued to focus on providing high-quality products that let their users record high-quality audio.

Pro Tools systems offer hardware options that are vast, expensive, and very powerful. They have built systems that integrate together and easily expand to whatever number of tracks and features you need. Digidesign has also addressed the needs of the entry-level market, creating specific systems that are inexpensive, offer most of the features new recordists could imagine having, and produce high-quality audio.

The brilliance of the Digidesign approach has been in using the same feel for the user interface across the board with all their products and making a marketing statement that they are the professional product of choice. Also, a number of years ago they started to offer a free version of the Pro Tools software. It wouldn't record many tracks and it was definitely limited in expandability and interface options, but it felt and looked just like the same Pro Tools used in world-class studios. Is that a great way to draw in the entry-level folks, or what? Of course, once these folks succeed and get some money to spend, they'll consider Pro Tools very seriously.

Digital Performer by Mark of the Unicorn (Mac)

Mark of the Unicorn (MOTU) was one of the first players on the block with Performer in the early eighties. They immediately had an edge over their competitors because, especially at that time, their user interface was far more intuitive and user-friendly than anyone else's around. They still have an amazing interface and produce an excellent product.

MOTU has always been a Mac product from its inception. They offer excellent and inexpensive hardware options as well. Their 2408 digital audio interfaces were immediately accepted and put to use making great music. They sounded good and cost less than $1000 at a time when competitors were charging much more for the same capabilities in their products.

MOTU was a leader in offering FireWire audio interfaces. They have done a good job of providing great software and affordable and powerful audio, MIDI, and synchronizing interfaces.

Nuendo and Cubase by Steinberg (Windows and Mac)

Cubase has been around for a while and has a large user base. Nuendo is a newer product and it instantly developed a loyal customer base. Being a Mac or Windows program, this Steinberg product serves a larger audience then Digital Performer. In addition, Nuendo became a leader in features soon after it was introduced—other manufacturers were scrambling to catch up, or at least to get their updates into circulation.

The Steinberg products offer excellent features and plenty of power to produce high-quality audio.

Cakewalk and Sonar by Twelve Tone Systems (Windows)

Cakewalk has been the entry-level software of choice for PC/Windows users. It is inexpensive and offers plenty of features to produce great music. Sonar is the new release from the Cakewalk folks and is more complex and powerful. This software has provided a platform for many talented PC owners to realize their creative vision. It's probably not the most powerful but it fills a need and does an excellent job.

Logic by Apple (Mac)

Logic Pro from Apple is the newest player among this crowd, although Logic was purchased by Apple from Emagic, who developed the essence of this program a number of years ago. Apple has made huge advancements in this package and in many ways is leading the industry in features and capabilities.

The fact that Apple is a computer manufacturer has given them an edge in integrating software with the CPU. Their shared processing, which allows for connecting multiple Power Macs via gigabit Ethernet or FireWire, is a very advanced audio recording procedure, which lets the user build a very powerful network of computers that act as one very fast and very powerful unit. Processing for multiple functions, such as plug-ins, large numbers of audio tracks, effects, and rendering, can be shared in real time across a powerful network.

Logic's inclusion of powerful virtual instruments in their core software is a leading feature, and the fact that the plug-ins actually sound good says a lot for Apple's desire to succeed in the music software arena.

Acid by Sony Media Software (Windows)

Sony Media Software's Acid is a very powerful loop-based program that also offers some audio recording capabilities. Being a Windows-only package, this single software package has tempted many loyal Mac users to buy a PC.

Sony Media Software provides an excellent tool for the production of good music with Acid. It provides drum loops that sound great and lead the industry in features. Their drum loops sound like real drums while still adjusting to the MIDI sequence tempo.

Features You Should Expect in Your Software

Intuitive User Interface

The look and feel of a software package is a very important part of the creative freedom you can expect to feel when using the software. This is all about music. It's not too difficult to tell the software that was designed by the technically minded with the intent of doing lots of tasks from software designed by musicians with the sole intent of providing a creative setting for producing great music.

You should expect an elegant graphical user interface (GUI– pronounced "Gooey"). If you look at the interface on your computer screen and you don't immediately see and understand the basic recording functions, try another package. Even though these packages have gotten very deep in their total capacity to produce current music, you still should be able to poke around without looking at a manual and get something to work.

MIDI Sequencer

MIDI is still a large part of current music production. In this era, the MIDI capacity of your software should be virtually limitless.

Multiple Options for Audio Interfaces

The software package is only the front end of the complete package. The actual audio must pass through some sort of interface. The interface contains A/D and D/A converters and allows for routing of audio channels and content in nearly any imaginable way. Most current software packages recognize several different audio and MIDI interfaces. Digidesign has been the most proprietary, although even they have opened up to more cross-platform compatibilities.

Ideally, you should select the software that feels most natural to your working style and combine it with the interface that precisely fits your needs.

Excellent Organizational Architecture

You'll be amazed at how demanding you get once you really get into your software. There are so many features that you'll end up using on a regular basis that navigational factors become unexpectedly critical to your creative success.

If you're continually lost in the maze and the way out is well hidden, you'll live in a state of frustration. On the other hand, sometimes you just have to learn your software—and you have to learn the audio recording procedure in general. I've worked on a lot of systems, and the systems I know, I know really well. Armed with the knowledge of the depth of one program, it's not that difficult to learn another program because you know what you're looking for. If you're new to recording in general, you'll need to spend a fair amount of time learning your system and the recording process.

Ideally, you'll have some knowledge of the recording process, and the menus, windows, and controls will be laid out in a way that makes sense to you and fits the way you produce music.

Look for features that help you keep your project organized as it builds. It's easy to add a lot of tracks in a project, especially considering MIDI and audio tracks. Your software should provide an easy way to group tracks together visually and physically. A simple feature like color-coding tracks is a time saver—it should just be there and it should be easy to figure out.

It's important that you're able to place markers throughout the song to tag the verses, choruses, bridge, solos, and any other musical section or visual cue. These markers are important to the flow of a project. It is counterproductive to be continually searching for a musical section—find it once, mark it, then go to the marker list next time you need to locate the section.

Several Editing Options

Event List

In the early days of digital editing, all we had to work with was the event list. This is a simple list of all the audio or MIDI events with a reference to the time they start, the time they end, and any MIDI data information you choose to view.

Video Example 2-1

The Event List in Action

Event List

Each MIDI event can be viewed on the Event List, a completely numerical table referencing MIDI events. Exact positions are referenced to a detailed timeline, whether measures and bars or hours, minutes, and seconds.

The Event List editor is an excellent tool for detailed tweaking of note position and length. Additionally, to change any parameter, simply double- or single-click on the corresponding number and type in a new value.

This isn't the easiest way to edit at first; however, once you're familiar with the numerical values and what they apply to musically, the Event List is a very efficient means of performing certain types of edits. For example, if you are polishing a MIDI piano recording and one note in a chord stciks out too much in the mix, open the Event List editor, find the note, double-click the velocity value, and type in a smaller number.

This tool also typically responds to the MIDI input device so changes can easily be made from the keyboard or other device. For instance, if you want to change a pitch, simply double-click the note in the list, play the correct note on the MIDI keyboard, and the note will be repaired.

Graphic Editor

A program called Master Tracks Pro made the Graphic editor popular. This editor represents each note or event with its own horizontal line that resides on a master timeline. This editor has a keyboard running vertically up the side of the window, and each note on the keyboard defines the MIDI note value of the vertical lines on the graph. A Graphic editor lets the user drag either end of the event to shorten or lengthen the note, or the line can be dragged up or down to change the note value.

Graphic Editor

The Graphic editor plots MIDI data on a timeline referenced to the notes on a piano keyboard. Double-click on the corresponding note value on the keyboard to highlight all events on that pitch throughout the sequence.

This is an excellent editor to use when adjusting drum and percussion grooves. Simply double-click on a drum note on the keyboard to select all the hits for that instrument in the sequence, then click and hold on any event. Drag up and down, and you'll hear the notes sound from each note. Drag to find the perfect snare sound and release the mouse—you've changed all the drum hits to another sound in no time.

Below the note grid, all note-on velocities are plotted and can be raised or lowered by simply dragging the indicators up or down.

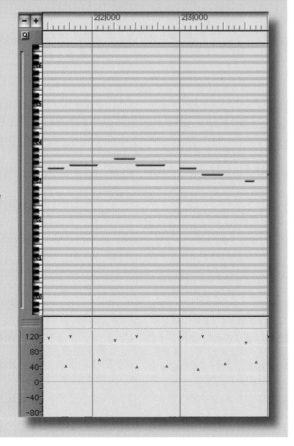

Video Example 2-2

Graphic Edit in Action

Notation Editor

To those who are musically schooled, the Notation editor is a powerful tool. All of your MIDI data prints out in musical notation. If you read music, it's easy to see a mistake in the notation window. If you find a wrong note, simply click on it and drag it into place—this applies to note value as well as rhythmic placement.

Video Example 2-3

The Notation Editor in Action

Notation Editor

The Notation editor is somewhat useless for those who don't read music. On the other hand, if you're a schooled musician this is an incredibly useful editor. Notes are printed out in sheet music form. If a sour note is found, simply drag it to the correct pitch. Notice the tool palette on the left side of the illustration. With these tools, notes can be added, pages can be titled, accidentals can be changed, and more. Depending on the software package you select, the Notation editor is capable of producing sheet music that can be used and read by a competent musician.

Drum Editor

The Drum editor feels a lot like the old Roland TR-808 on steroids. The drum groove is laid out on a grid, with the rhythmic subdivision (quarter notes, eighth notes, sixteenth notes, etc.) divided evenly across the x-axis and the pitches (drums and percussion instruments) listed along the y-axis. If the grid is empty there's no groove. When you click on the grid, the box fills in and the instrument you've selected plays on the beat you've selected. This is a very useful tool for fine-tuning drum grooves because you just need to click on a note and drag it to another box on the grid.

Video Example 2-4

The Drum Editor in Action

Drum Editor

The Drum editor provides an excellent bird's-eye view of the drum pattern. To change an instrument or a beat, simply drag the block to another square. The grid represents all the beats of the rhythmic background unit. This is an excellent tool to set up the groove. Create a loop the length of your basic groove pattern, hit play, and start fine-tuning the rhythmic essence of your track. This visual representation of the drum pattern, feels like the vintage Roland TR-808 drum machine—it was based on the same type of rhythmic grid.

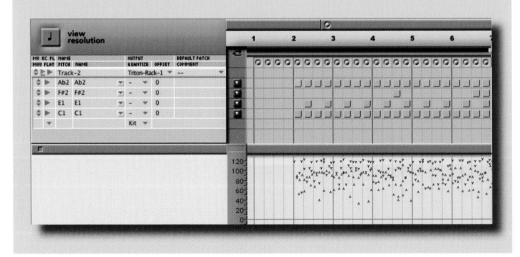

Waveform Editor

The audio Waveform editor provides a graphic view of the audio waveform along with all the tools you can imagine for cutting, copying, pasting, stretching, squeezing, duplicating, and positioning. There are also typically tools available to change tuning, timbre, and, using the plug-in library, virtually anything about the waveform.

Video Example 2-5

The Waveform Editor in Action

Waveform Editor

The Waveform editor displays the actual variance in amplitude over time that produces sound. With this editor you can actually see where the words and sounds start and stop.

This is the most useful tool for editing voice, whether singing or voice-over. In fact, any track is easy to edit because of the visual cues provided by the sound waves.

The zoom feature magnifies the view from a general overview of several minutes all the way into a portion of one cycle of one wave. The illustration to the right demonstrates zooming in on a portion of a waveform. In the closest view, the pencil tool can actually redraw the amplitude variations of the sound wave. This is useful in getting rid of an unwanted click or pop. Keep zooming in until you find the click, then just draw through it to eliminate the unwanted sound.

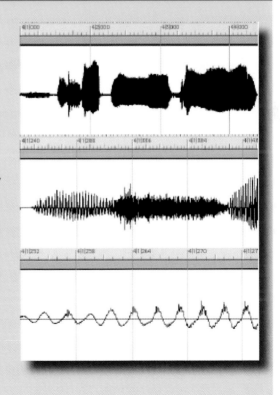

Mixer

There should be an on-screen mixer that contains very similar features and layout to a hardware mixer. The use of this mixer must be intuitive and easy to navigate. On-screen mixer channels typically contain all the regular controls: fader, pan, mute, bus assignments, and aux send level controls. Additionally, they'll likely contain mix automation controls, surround controls (when activated), and several insert boxes for inserting plug-ins into the digital signal path.

Software mixers don't typically contain dedicated equalization controls because EQ is usually selected from a list of several types of EQ plug-ins available, either as part of the host application or from third-party plug-in manufacturers.

The Mixer

The virtual mixer in your software package is very much like a physical mixer. Faders control listening levels; pan controls sweep from left to right; aux sends feed effects and buses; mutes switch the channel on and off; solo buttons focus on the selected tracks only; record-enable buttons ready the record process; and inserts provide access to the signal path for use with dynamic control or effects.

Most software mixers are easy to use, although many engineers prefer the look and feel of a physical device. Because of this fact, most audio equipment manufacturers make a tactile control surface. This device looks like a normal physical mixer but it controls software parameters, typically via MIDI communication protocol.

These mixers control both MIDI and digital audio tracks.

Video Example 2-6

The Software Mixer in Action

Automation

Automation is usually available in a couple different configurations and should control both the audio and MIDI tracks.

1. The mixer typically contains automation write and playback buttons. These are really very simple to use. Just select write mode before you make a channel change, and the change you make will be written into the automation data. When you rewind the song and play it back, the change you made will happen automatically.

2. You can also automate in the waveform window of most software packages. This automation system is graphic rather than motion-based. In the mixer, we see the fader move or the pan control turn, and so on. In this graphic mode the parameter changes are drawn in by adjusting the height of a horizontal line. This is a very powerful and convenient way to automate.

We will eventually see the great capacity and power of automation. The fundamentals of this subject are very simple, but the automation process is very important and deep.

Video Example 2-7

Software Automation in Action

Data Conversion In and Out

Most current software provides an easy way to convert data from one digital format to another. Data should be the same sample format (bit rate and sample rate) in order to function within one recording—if your recording is at 24-bit, 96 kHz, all the ingredients should either be recorded at or converted to 24/96. Typically, this is mandatory for functionality, but even if simultaneous playback of multiple formats is an option, it doesn't make sense to waste processor power on real-time conversion. You'll simply overtax the processor and/or get less than perfect data format conversion.

Additionally, there must be a way to export your audio into a common playback format. Whether AIFF, MP3, AAC, WAV, or whatever the current format du jour is, this export should be simple, fast, and obvious.

MIDI Effects Plug-Ins

MIDI effects plug-ins typically offer basic delays, dynamic compression and expansion, arpeggiation, time shift, transposition, as well as various continuous data adjustments. These effects don't have the scope of audio effects because MIDI data is all numerical performance data. There's no audio in MIDI data, just triggers to start, stop, and alter MIDI events within a MIDI device.

Audio Effects Plug-Ins

Software packages include basic plug-in effects. These are a good sampling of the fundamental effects you need to get most of the basic sounds you hear on your favorite recordings.

The third-party after-market effect is where you get to personalize your digital studio. The software package you buy provides everything you need to get started. However, as you solidify what your musical and functional style is, adding the plug-ins that really promote your type of musical creativity provides powerful inspiration and facilitates the growth of your personal style.

Audio plug-ins provide every effect you can imagine in several different forms. Effects plug-ins don't all sound the same. Everything depends on the complexity and efficiency of the algorithm (the math behind the effect). Each EQ sounds a little different, reverberation algorithms vary greatly, and dynamics controls create an amazingly different sound quality. Waves has been producing excellent-sounding and very powerful plug-ins for a long time. TC Electronics offers plug-ins that are accompanied by hardware, which adds processing power through a FireWire connection. Universal Audio is a vintage company that has manufactured many of the classic and most highly respected tools in the audio industry. They make plug-ins that mirror the sonic quality of their vintage equipment, like the 1176 and LA2A—it's really very amazing. I still use their vintage gear and I also use their plug-ins. The sonic similarity is uncanny.

MIDI and Audio Transposition

With a simple MIDI file, transposition to a new key has always been simple—just copy the data from one key and automatically transpose it to a new key. Current software should be able to perform the same task with both MIDI and audio. If you want to modulate a song by repeating the chorus a whole step higher at the end, you should be able to perform that task automatically by copying the chorus and selecting Transpose from the menu. It should sound natural and be virtually undetectable on all single-note tracks, such as vocals or other instruments that play one note at a time. Your audio transposition should control both pitch and formants (note value and tone quality). It should be able to change the pitch within a certain tolerance and maintain the original tone quality. If you don't have this separate control, the vocals might suddenly sound younger or like Alvin and the Chipmunks.

Audio transposition is only growing into its ability to perform transposition on complex, multi-note audio. This is typically a hit-or-miss event.

Beat Detection and Automatic Alignment

Your software should allow you to define alignment positions that you can force your audio segments to align with. There should also be a beat detection scheme that analyzes the audio waveforms for transients, indicating the beat structure of your music.

There should also be a way to resolve real-time rhythms to the MIDI tempo and beat grid. In other words, you should be able to record a drum track that's a little out of the pocket and have the computer automatically align it to the groove of your choice.

Multiple Synchronization Options

The beauty and the disdain of digital systems is that they can all work together as one unit. They can synchronize through a sample accurate word clock so that every time the master system moves one sample ahead, the slave systems move ahead one sample. This is excellent, although it doesn't always work without some hair pulling. It's really gotten a lot better in recent years but it's still the one thing my buddies call for help with the most. I can typically get their systems up and working relatively quickly, but it's only because I've spent a lot of time being *very* frustrated with this topic. The theory isn't difficult but the application across multiple platforms is often troublesome.

Your software should sync to word clock, ADAT sync, standard beat clock, MIDI Time Code, direct time lock, and to MIDI triggers from any MIDI note value. It should also possess the capacity to resolve to any frame rate (30, 29.97, 24 fps, with or without drop frame, etc.).

Multiple Quantizing Options

Quantizing basically resolves an event to a time grid. The simplest quantization resolves MIDI notes to a user-selected background unit like eighth or sixteenth notes. No matter where you rhythmically play a note it will be drawn to the closest background unit. Current software offers variations in grid that are not simply mathematically perfect subdivisions of a measure. You get to choose from preset grooves where certain beats are ahead or behind the beat, or you can design your own groove by selecting the rhythmic position of each beat. Then the quantization engine automatically conforms all events to that grid, rather than the mathematically perfect grid.

There also should be capabilities to adjust the severity of conformation. This strength control is like a magnet that is adjustable in strength. At 100 percent it drags every event exactly to the grid, at 50 percent it only draws the events 50 percent of the way to the grid, and so on.

Easy Archival of Files

When you're backing up a project or saving for archival you must be sure that you're saving everything associated with your music. It's possible that you've imported audio from another file or that a drive was temporarily unavailable during recording and some of your audio data ended up at another location than the project audio file. If this has happened (and yes, it does happen), you might save your project, then a couple years later when you need to recall it for a remix or some other label purpose, half the audio is missing. Ouch!

Your software must have an easy and intuitive way to gather all the files that are part of your project, saving them to one location. This feature is typically in the File menu and is labeled Save as a Copy, or Save As, with an option to save all audio with the file. Always do this when you archive or back up projects.

Provision for Most Hardware Control Surfaces

Software today needs to have an option to receive control commands from an external control surface. To those who are used to working with a physical mixer, one of the biggest frustrations of software-based recording is the lack of faders and knobs. Several manufacturers offer controllers with a real tactile feel that support most popular DAWs. These tactile control surfaces can greatly increase your efficiency.

Easy Integration of Pre-Recorded Loops

As a drummer and player for most of my life I was a reluctant participant in the world of loops. Although I still love recording custom parts played by real people, made up specifically for one song, loops have evolved into a very useful tool—indeed, they are just another tool in the musician's belt.

Your software must have an easy interface for the integration of loops. The loops should automatically play at the project tempo, and they should retain their sonic quality no matter what the tempo. Much of the responsibility for these features resides in the accompanying plug-ins, but no matter what, there should be facilitation for incorporating prerecorded loops.

Virtual Instrument Capabilities

Virtual instruments are a huge part of the music production industry. As recordists you need to use software with easy and intuitive capacity for virtual instruments. A *virtual instrument* is essential a software sound module. All the processing power comes from your CPU. These tools are very useful and sonically superior. The processor in today's computer is several times more powerful than the processor in a sound module or keyboard.

The downside of a virtual instrument is in the drain it puts on your CPU. If you use several virtual instruments while recording a lot of audio tracks, you better have a very fast and powerful computer.

Surround Sound Support

Surround sound is with us to stay; your software should have the capacity to mix in surround up to 7.1. High-definition audio formats like DVD-Audio and SACD are at least predecessors of the future of audio. You should pay attention to the surround phenomenon and you should gear up to produce surround mixes in HD audio.

Download Demos

Many of the current software packages are available online or via mail as demos. They either stop working after a specified period of time or they have limited functionality of a particular feature such as saving, exporting, and so on.

No matter what anyone says about a package, there's nothing like opening it up and seeing what comes naturally for you, then pressing in further to see just how it can help you live a creatively unencumbered life.

You should try before you buy.

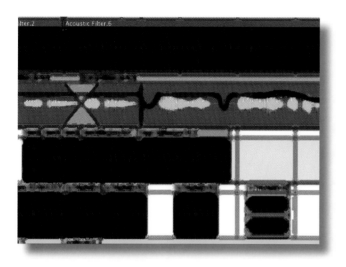

Digital Editing

Tape recorders became a reality in the mid-1950s. They offered a feature that had previously been either prohibitively cumbersome or impossible: Whatever was recorded on tape could be edited, moved around, or tightened up. Separate takes could even be pieced together. As radio was increasing in size and power, any tool that would help speed up production and increase quality was destined to make its mark.

Bing Crosby was the first real celebrity to try this new medium. He was frustrated with the lack of flexibility in the 78 RPM recording process. Using tape, he could record his radio programs, cutting out mistakes, ill-chosen words, or unacceptable performances. Magnetic tape, an engineer, and a box of razor blades gave him control over production quality and provided a reliable medium for storage.

Digital editing, also referred to as *random access editing*, has given us a new level of control over production quality, and the digital storage medium has proven to be reliable, affordable, and flexible.

Early digital editing systems were very expensive and the storage medium was either prohibitively costly or it was *slow!* One of the first digital systems I worked with archived short samples to a standard 5 1/4-inch floppy disk. In the operation manual, the manufacturer suggested that the time while the data was being saved could be used for such tasks as learning to fly an airliner or becoming a brain surgeon! They weren't far off.

Current systems are fast, and the storage media is cheap. Very cool!

The Basics

Most digital editing systems utilize similar terminology. In addition, many parameters, functions, and controls are alike in basic design. There are only so many functions to perform; the course of time and competition has brought technological processes closer and closer together in their performance and practical functionality. The simple fact that competitors in the industry watch each other and copy whoever has the hot hand of the day has an impact on the corporate development of standards. We've definitely seen this phenomenon in the MIDI sequencer manufacturers, and the same thing is happening with the digital editing systems.

Whether or not the recording platform you're operating on uses these exact terms, make yourself familiar with them. As fast as technology changes, you'll probably see these features and functions come across your computer screen soon.

Nondestructive Editing

Nearly all edits performed in modern digital editors are nondestructive. Nondestructive editing has no adverse effect on the original waveform.

No audio data is ever written or destroyed in the nondestructive digital editing procedure. Audio, which exists on the hard drive, is merely referenced and accessed, leaving the actual data untouched.

Creating a nondestructive data file affords the user the luxury of reordering musical sections, dialogue, or sound effects in as many ways as he or she can envision. All this is available in an environment that results in no degradation at all to audio quality.

Since this process is only referencing existing audio, it has little effect on the size of a digital audio file. The only thing being written in a nondestructive edit is the reference to the data location on the drive, along with reference to in and out points. So, hundreds of edits can be written in one file with little relative increase in file size.

Destructive Editing

Destructive editing changes and replaces the original waveform, rendering the original irretrievable. This type of editing is rare, though most packages provide a way to perform it. Fortunately, destructive editing normally requires specific actions, procedures, or keystrokes that the user must consciously perform in order for the destructive edit to finalize.

Pencil edits, where the actual waveform is redrawn by the operator, are destructive, though they can be undone immediately after the action if the desired results aren't achieved.

Whenever sections of audio are removed in a destructive way, the computer processor must recalculate the positioning of data, therefore taxing the processor and requiring a fair amount of time. Depending on the speed of your computer system and the amount of data after the edit, this type of destructive editing could take several minutes.

Regions

A *region* is simply a defined section of a waveform. If you've just recorded the lead vocal track in one continuous pass, the entire track could be called a region. If you highlight the first chorus, you can specifically define that highlighted area as a separate region. Typically, once you've defined or created a region, it shows up on a list of regions, which can be inserted into a playlist at any time. Once a region is defined, it can be named, marked, and edited. New regions can be made from within any region.

Regions can be used repeatedly, if needed. Using a region multiple times takes up no more disk space than just using it once, since the region name simply refers to a specified portion of data located at one point on the drive. Creating and changing regions is a completely nondestructive procedure.

Selecting Regions

The light-blue shaded area of the waveform below is a selected region. A region can be any specified portion of a song, track, take, etc. During the digital recording process, there are many times when it's necessary to choose a specific audio portion, or region, to process in different ways. In this case, the region is selected by double-clicking the waveform view, then dragging across the desired area.

Regions are also selected by numerically defining a range of measures, or time, then selecting a group of tracks—in this case, the region is defined across all selected tracks.

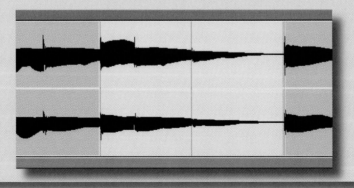

Playlist/Edit Decision List

A *playlist* is exactly what it sounds like. It's a list indicating the playback order for specified regions. The playlist is an essential tool in most digital editing packages. Recorders based on specific hardware with a single access window often use a playlist that scrolls in a vertical manner, usually referred to as an *edit decision list*, or *EDL*.

A playlist is usually characterized by waveform graphics onscreen, whereas an EDL, in its vertically scrolling list, utilizes text, indicating the track name, as well as in and out points for each list item. These in and out locators are referenced to time code. Crossfade, loop, and playback level information is often included in the EDL. The EDL can be a very convenient way to keep track of certain types of audio programs. Film and video hit points for sound effects are often easy to track this way.

Most software-based systems display the playlist along a horizontal timeline, with visual representations of the waveforms scrolling from left to right. In this type of editor, one region naturally flows into the next and they connect, butt together, or crossfade graphically in a way that's easy to understand.

Playlists utilizing graphic representations of each waveform are very user-friendly. Almost anybody can jump into this process and instantly understand what's going on. Once a few terms and tools are understood, editing proceeds in a logical and easy to understand manner.

RAM Buffer

In order for a hard disk-based editing system to keep up with the demands of random access editing, a storage area for backlogging data is needed. No drive is fast enough to provide continual instant access to regions of audio data, especially as they hop from sector to sector on

Edit Decision List

The edit decision list (EDL) is a very convenient way to edit audio segment start and end positions. Once you get used to it, this can be the most efficient manner to adjust audio segment timing. Although it isn't as graphic as some screens, it is very efficient.

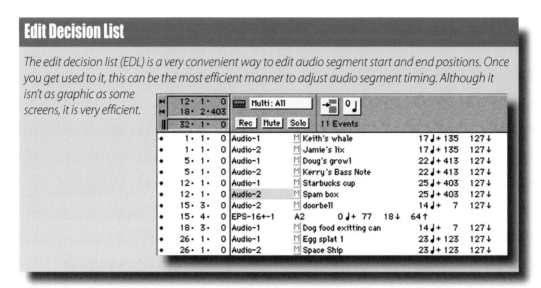

the drive. Therefore, a clever scheme, like that used by the MiniDisc, allows data to pass into a RAM buffer before it actually flows in the data signal path. Data flows into the RAM buffer—in the correct order for playback—and is streamed out of the buffer, after a slight delay, at the proper rate.

This process is like filling a bucket of water with a hole in the bottom. It buys the drive some time to find a specified portion of audio, stream it into the RAM buffer, then repeat the activity for all the items on the EDL or playlist. The buffer flows the digital data stream at the proper rate and in the user-determined order seamlessly.

Gain Change/Normalizing

Gain change is a very simple concept. It applies to digital and analog audio in the same ways. When increasing the gain in either format, you're simply turning the level of everything up or down; the effect of the gain change is global for the selected audio. In analog, you turn the level control up or down. In the computer-based digital domain, the processor simply adds or subtracts equal amounts of level from each sample.

Normalizing is a type of gain change used in the digital domain. The computer searches the selected waveform for its peak amplitude, then equally adjusts each sample in the wave so that the peak is at maximum amplitude. Some software packages include a percentage parameter in their normalize screen, and the user can adjust the waveform so that the peak is at a certain percentage of maximum amplitude.

We know that when the full amplitude is utilized in the digital waveform we're using all of the available bits. In addition, we know that when only half the available amplitude is used in digital audio we've only really used half our available resolution, or bits. Therefore, it makes sense that adjusting the waveform gain to maximum, or normalizing, would be the right thing to do for the sake of audio integrity and efficient use of the available audio bits. In some instances, this theory holds true; in others it doesn't.

Normalizing Low-Level Digital Recordings

Waveform A represents a properly recorded digital audio segment. Waveform B is the same example as waveform A, recorded at an extremely low digital level. Waveform C show a 100 percent normalization of waveform B. Notice how the basic waveform shape has been built in waveform C. However, the fine detail and precision have obviously not been identically rebuilt through the process. Audio Examples 3-1 though 3-3 show the sonic correlation to the graphics in this illustration.

Most audio purists avoid normalization because of the inaccuracy of the simple mathematical transformation. The best idea is to record levels as full as possible without overloading.

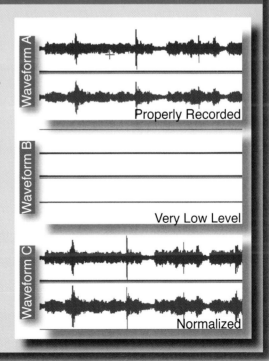

Waveform A — Properly Recorded

Waveform B — Very Low Level

Waveform C — Normalized

As the processor calculates gain changes from low-level signals, we run into problems. In the digital domain, low-level signals are best left that way. The resolution in very low-level signals is also very low, so when the gain is changed the result is simply a louder version of a low-level, low-resolution sound. Increasing the gain of poorly recorded audio does not increase the resolution. If you only use six bits of a 24-bit word and then turn up the level to occupy the space of a full 24-bit signal, the resulting audio doesn't sound like 24 bits. It sounds like a loud six-bit waveform.

The very best solution to this normalizing process is to record your original audio as close as possible to maximum amplitude. In this way, the only sounds recorded at very low levels are sounds meant to be there. In terms of waveform amplitude, the only way to optimize the clarity of your digital recordings is to use the full amount of available amplitude.

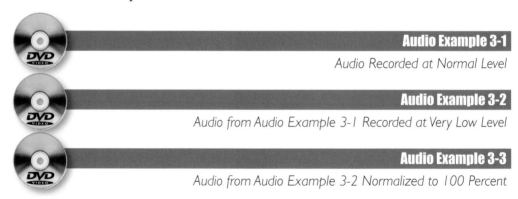

Audio Example 3-1
Audio Recorded at Normal Level

Audio Example 3-2
Audio from Audio Example 3-1 Recorded at Very Low Level

Audio Example 3-3
Audio from Audio Example 3-2 Normalized to 100 Percent

Cut, Copy, and Paste

It's very efficient and convenient that computer-based digital editing software packages utilize many of the same commands as other software. Cut, Copy, Paste, Undo, Redo, Save, and so on are typically performed the same way they are in most word processing, spreadsheet, or database software—and often with the same keystrokes.

The nondestructive digital editor doesn't move data in these functions; it merely references sections of previously existing data. Therefore, all these functions are nearly instantaneous. To move or remove a section requires no waiting. Once you select a region and execute a command, it's done. This is an amazing leap ahead from the analog domain.

The addition of these simple computer functions raises the efficiency of the recording process by incredible amounts. The fact that a large chorus with several difficult vocal parts can be perfected within seconds, copied and pasted into every chorus section, is amazing when compared to the alternative. This feature alone could save hours on one song!

Undo, Redo, Save, Revert to Saved

The Undo command could be the single most important feature in computer-based digital recording—at least it seems like it when you've mistakenly erased a sax solo played by a high-priced virtuoso who's no longer in the country.

Erasing a track or several tracks by mistake is one of the worst feelings in the recording process. (Can you feel my personal pain here?) Once it's gone, it's gone! No amount of weeping, gnashing of teeth, apologizing, or groveling can bring it back.

But the Undo command saves the day. The computer-based digital recorder lets you undo your last action. So, if you realize that you just taped over the lead vocal track with that triangle part, simply press Undo and the lead vocal lives again! It's an amazing feeling: like finding a lost puppy, realizing you didn't just run over your vintage Les Paul in your car, or realizing that girl making out with Bruno on the beach is somebody else's daughter.

If you undo a recording or other action and then you realize you shouldn't have undone it, you can use the Redo command to redo it. If you finish recording a vocal track and, in your infinite wisdom, decide it was garbage and nobody on the planet will ever want to hear it, you can simply undo or cut the take in order to save disk space. Then, when the vocalist starts exclaiming how great the take was and how he could never sing it that well again, you can quietly and calmly press the Redo command. This is a good era to be alive in!

Remember, anytime a computer is involved, save often! Saving is part of my regular functionality—like breathing. In fact, I just saved. Crashes happen and data gets lost, so save a lot. Some programs have auto-save features. Sometimes that's good and sometimes it's not. The only time I avoid saving is when I try something that involves moving sections of music around. Within a few minutes an arrangement can be tested in different forms and then, if no forward progress is made, I can select Return to Saved. This feature closes down the file and reopens it in its most recently saved form.

Save As/Save a Copy As

If your arrangement is sounding good, but you'd like to try something different and you're not sure whether it will improve or ruin your music, try saving the file as a different name. This way you get to keep the status of your song intact, so you can come back to it if your experiment is a flop.

Use the Save As command to save your song as another file under another name. I like to save by the same name with a different revision number. For example, "My Song rev. 1.1" or "My Song rev. 2.0" is easy to distinguish from "My Song." Try using the same kind of system for numbering revisions that the software manufacturers use for their upgrades. A minor revision gets an increase only to the right of the decimal point; major revisions see a change to the left of the decimal point.

Save As is different from Save a Copy As. Save As simply creates another document icon and a new program file, but all audio continues to be referenced from its original audio folders.

Save a Copy As not only saves the program file icon as a different name, it also saves all referenced audio files into a new folder. It's very difficult to archive a song with several audio sound files without a feature like Save a Copy As. Sometimes, a sound file that's referenced in your data file never makes it into the folder with the rest of the sound files. This can happen when you import audio from another file, or if you've saved a copy as a different name—or sometimes it seems like it's just an inside joke that the computer gets a real kick out of. Use Save a Copy As any time you want to create a new file containing all audio data related to a specific song. Whether archiving or transporting, if you need to be sure you have all necessary files, use this command.

Waveform/Pencil Editing

Most digital editing packages provide a facility for waveform editing, sometimes referred to as *pencil editing*. The pencil tool lets the user destructively redraw waveform data. It's necessary to zoom in to the sample level where just a single line wave is seen onscreen. Once zoomed in far enough, the pencil tool becomes accessible.

Since this is a destructive edit, pre-plan your edits to avoid causing more problems than you repair. This technique is commonly used to repair clicks, pops, and other erroneous transients. These glitches can be seen onscreen as sharp and protruding spikes. They are easily repaired by zooming in, accessing the pencil tool, and redrawing the wave at the questionable point.

Sometimes the spike still looks like a spike in closeup view, and sometimes it doesn't. Often, the waveform that results in a spike in zoomed-out view is really a tightly grouped series of small peaks. The appearance of these grouped peaks can be deceiving in closeup view. However, they're often grouped conspicuously closer together than the surrounding crests and troughs. Redrawing over these grouped peaks to form one wave that occupies the same space as the entire group often solves this problem.

Smoothing

Smoothing is another technique that works very well when an erroneous peak occurs. This is very similar to editing with the pencil tool. Simply zoom in on the peak in question, then highlight it. When the smoothing task is requested, the processor calculates a smoother wave for the selected area. This technique usually works very well. If for some reason

Repairing Clicks, Pops, and Spikes

Waves A, B, C, and D show the repair of a particular pop within a digital audio segment. Notice the peak in A. When zoomed in to view the wave, we might expect to see one big peak. However, often the peak comes from a small grouping (B). The energy accumulates in a small region to additively form a large mass of energy. To repair this type of pop or click, simply use the pencil tool to draw a smooth wave in the place of the jagged ones (C). Often, this procedure seamlessly eliminates the noise.

it doesn't, undo the action, change the selected area to include more or less of the waveform, and try again.

Some smoothing plug-ins provide user-adjustable parameters. Some simply smooth the selected area according to preset guidelines. This is a very convenient feature that typically works very well with little tweaking, as long as you've selected the correct portion of the waveform.

Preview Mode

Preview mode lets the user hear what an edit or other digital manipulation sounds like before committing to the change. Preview often allows you to hear crossfades before okaying them.

When using plug-ins or other effects that either create a new waveform or permanently alter the existing waveform, preview mode is almost always available. Devices that include real-time effects don't have a need for preview mode because they allow effects to be altered at any time without any change to the original waveform.

Fades

In the analog world, fades are preformed manually through VCA automation or, at best, moving fader automation. There is definitely an art to the manual fade. Many excellent recordings have faded out (or in) at the hand of the mixing engineer. In most VCA and moving fader automation packages, it's possible to let the computer fade in or out according to a user-defined fade length.

Computer-controlled digital fades are very flexible, smooth, and easy. The length of the fade can be determined by setting the length of the fade onscreen or by highlighting the area the fade should occupy. Typically, digital fades can be shaped or drawn within the software package.

Computer-Assisted Fades

A lot of great music has been faded out by an engineer painstakingly lowering the master fader level. It can be done. However, the digitally facilitated and automated fade is very smooth; it can be tweaked to a very fine degree and it can be duplicated as many times as needed. Computer-assisted fades are especially useful for feathering out the end portion of a song, where the manual fader resolution at the bottom of the fader throw makes it difficult to finish the fade.

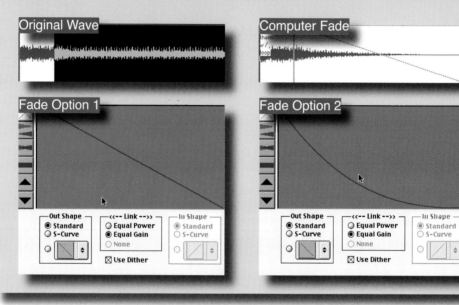

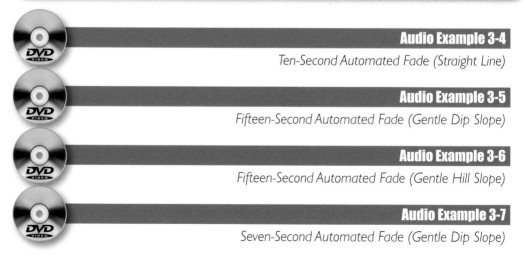

Audio Example 3-4

Ten-Second Automated Fade (Straight Line)

Audio Example 3-5

Fifteen-Second Automated Fade (Gentle Dip Slope)

Audio Example 3-6

Fifteen-Second Automated Fade (Gentle Hill Slope)

Audio Example 3-7

Seven-Second Automated Fade (Gentle Dip Slope)

Crossfades

Prior to the availability of digital editing and features like the cross-fade, editing was performed on the master analog tape. The editor, by necessity, was very careful with every cut—the process wasn't nearly as casual as the digital-era editing process. When you're cutting the mixed master tape and there's no backup, every cut must be calculated and planned with great precision. A good tape editor constantly listens for the perfect hole in which to make the cut. All sounds are considered, including cymbal decay, reverb decay, every instrument's sustain, room sound, and instrumentation. Once everything has been considered and it looks like you've spotted the perfect edit point, it's time to make the cut, put the tape back together with special editing tape, then listen. Razor-blade editing is an art form that takes practice and patience. In the thousands of razor-blade edits I've made, I made very few irreparable errors, but I have spent a fair amount of time fixing questionable or downright awful edits. Therefore, I have great appreciation for the digital editing process.

The *crossfade*, simply an overlap of one region's fadeout with the next region's fade-in, is an amazingly useful tool that's available only in the digital domain. With this one tool, you can regularly perform smooth and undetectable edits that simply weren't possible before its introduction. A crossfade lets the recordist pick an edit point between two musical sections, then fade into one section while fading out of the other.

There are several types of crossfades; each has a place in digital editing that serves a unique function. In application, where one fade type results in a perfectly smooth and unnoticeable fade, another type might not work at all. As you practice applying the different types of fades, you'll soon develop a feel for which type produces the best results for each task. However, even the most experienced engineer needs to experiment with various options for certain more troublesome edit points.

The *edit point*, where two regions come together, might create a pop or click; one wave might be at the peak of its crest, for example, while the other is at the bottom of its trough. The ultimate goal of a crossfade is to smooth over an edit point so it's undetectable. Listeners should never be able to tell that the audio they hear has any edits, unless there's a musically creative reason to include the sound of two sections of audio butting together.

Digital edits, including fades and crossfades, are nondestructive unless you specifically choose to make them destructive. The edit point can easily be changed and the original unedited waveform is always available in case things ever get really messed up. In addition, digital edits can be fine-tuned later. It's possible to rough a task in, verifying time or musical flow, and then later focus in on the edit points in order to perfect each one.

Crossfading an Awkward Point

The edit point, where two regions come together, might create a pop or click; one wave might be at the peak of its crest, for example, while the other is at the bottom of its trough. The ultimate goal of a crossfade is to smooth over an edit point so it's undetectable. Listeners should never be able to tell that the audio they hear has any edits unless there's a musically creative reason to include the sound of two sections of audio butting together.

Linear Fade

Conceptually, the simplest crossfade is the linear fade; it uses a straight fadeout at the same time as a straight fade-in. Many digital editing systems utilize a linear crossfade on every edit to help smooth the transition from one region to the next. The fade duration is typically 10 ms or less—unnoticeable in terms of audible fade time—and is often user-definable.

A user-controlled linear fade is often 50 to 100 ms in length, though each edit is unique and requires evaluation as to its requirements. Special effects fades might be very long on both sides, but the limiting factor is

Linear Crossfade

The linear crossfade includes a straight ramp down from one audio segment in the same time period as a straight ramp up from the next audio segment. These are very common crossfades and they typically perform flawlessly. In fact, many workstations automatically include a five- to 10-millisecond crossfade on every edit, just to smooth over the point where differing audio butts together.

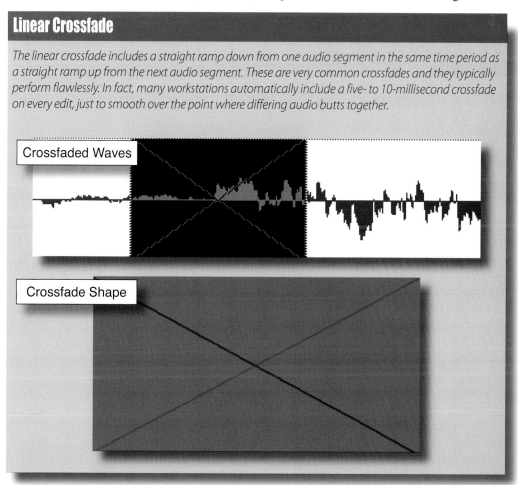

Crossfaded Waves

Crossfade Shape

processing power. Fades are a DSP-driven feature. Therefore, total fade length is dependent on available RAM and DSP power.

Audio Example 3-8

Awkward-Sounding Edit Point (No Crossfade)

Audio Example 3-9

Linear Crossfade of Audio Example 3-8

Curve Fade

The curve fade swoops in and up or down and out. This gentle curved crossfade works well in an application where the audio must enter and exit the crossfade zone gently. Crossfades with longer durations often produce very smooth music fades. The primary concern when utilizing linear or curve fades is a possible dip at the edit point. When this happens, an S-curve, equal power, or equal gain fade might produce a better fade.

S-Curve

The S-curve fades in faster at the start of the waveform and slower at the end. This type of fade curve is particularly useful for material that's difficult to crossfade. It typically helps to eliminate a drop in volume that sometimes occurs at the edit point when a linear or curve fade is used.

Audio Example 3-10

Awkward-Sounding Edit Point (No Crossfade)

Audio Example 3-11

S-Curve Crossfade of Audio Example 3-10

S-Curve Crossfades

The S-curve fades in faster at the start of the waveform and slower at the end. This type of fade curve is particularly useful for material that's difficult to crossfade. It typically helps to eliminate a drop in volume that sometimes occurs at the edit point when a linear or curve fade is used.

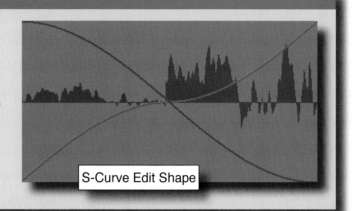

S-Curve Edit Shape

Overlap Fade

The overlap fade is characterized by an immediate rise in level at the beginning of the fade zone from the waveform fading in and an immediate drop in level of the wave at the end of the fade zone. Both regions maintain full amplitude throughout the fade. This type of fade works well when working from one ambient sound to another, especially when they're both behind other more important audio. The overlap fade doesn't usually work well for musical crossfades because the combined amplitude of two full-strength waveforms often produces dramatic peaks. If two musical sections fade in and out naturally, the overlap fade could be the perfect choice.

Equal Gain

A linear crossfade often produces a noticeable dip in level as one region fades into the next. Most software packages provide a means to link the fade curves in a way that maintains equal combined gain throughout the crossfade region. The equal gain fade works best when fading between two regions that sound alike—i.e., that are nearly phase-coherent. It also keeps a lid on the level, which helps to eliminate clipping when the equal power link might allow clipping.

Equal Power

This fade is best used when fading between two completely different-sounding regions. It links the two regions together in a way that continually analyzes the amount of energy created by the two regions. The software calculates the combined amplitude so that it maintains equal power throughout the fade range.

Pre-Roll/Post-Roll

In the computer-based digital domain, there is no waiting for tape to rewind or fast forward. If you need to return to the beginning of a song, it happens immediately, whether the song is 10 seconds or 100 minutes. However, it's not always efficient to locate to a specific edit point; it's usually best to start a few seconds before the edit and then listen over the edit, stopping a few seconds after the edit.

The amount of playback time prior to the edit point is called *pre-roll*; the amount of playback time after the edit point is called *post-roll*. These terms are commonly used in the video editing world, where the video tape actually rolls to a specified point ahead of the edit before it begins playback and then rolls after the edit point by the specified post-roll time.

Typical pre- and post-roll times are about three seconds. These parameters usually pertain to preview modes only, though some systems implement a pre-roll every time the transport locates an assigned position.

Online/Offline

Online and *offline* are terms used to denote a digital editor, tape recorder, or other device's status regarding synchronization.

A device that's online will receive and follow the synchronization master device. When the master begins playback, any device that's online immediately locates to the same point in the recording and plays along in sync.

A device that's offline is set to reference playback to its own internal clock, ignoring any other sync reference.

When operating a system that has several devices referencing a master sync source, it's common to go online and offline with a particular device. For example, in a setup including a computer and some ADATs, it's often convenient to take the computer offline to check some MIDI keyboard parts. It's usually a lot quicker and simpler to check parts on one device alone than it is to wait for all synchronized devices to find each other and then to check a part with everything running in sync.

Editing within the Software-Based Multitrack Domain

Many of the features used by the software-based digital editor are available on the newer modular digital multitracks, like those made by Alesis, Tascam, Fostex, and others. However, the most flexible multi-track platforms are computer-based, hard disk systems. The terms in this section apply specifically to computer-based systems, though many of them transfer to MDM systems. References to specific functions are not intended to be specific to any particular manufacturer.

Sound Files

Audio recorded to a hard disk recorder writes directly to the drive. It stays in that form unless the recordist decides to undo the recording or perform a destructive edit. The audio data is typically catalogued on a list of sound files, also called, among other things, *soundbites, waveforms, audio events, audio instruments,* or *audio files.*

When using a tape-based multitrack, a track is recorded and archived on tape until it's recorded over. Once you record over a tape track, it's gone forever.

In contrast to a tape-based recorder, once audio data is stored on the drive and catalogued in the audio file list, it remains there—even if the user cuts it from the playlist or EDL. Only a blatantly destructive edit removes audio from the drive, and the software will typically ask once or twice if the audio should really be erased from the drive. Other than saving disk space, there's not normally a good reason to destroy audio data. The fact that it remains on a list provides the user with the option to recall the audio any time.

Since all audio that's ever recorded in a session is available at any time, digital multitrack recording offers an amazing amount of flexibility. If the lead vocal track is just about perfect, there's really no risk in trying it again, recording right over the top of the original track. At any time, the older, almost perfect track can be recalled just as if it had never been cut.

Waveform View

Most editing and recording packages display audio data in a graphic waveform. This waveform shows exactly what the sound is doing. If it gets louder, the waveform gets bigger; if there's silence, the waveform display is a straight line. Editing becomes nearly as visual as it is aural.

The following illustration demonstrates how easy choosing an edit point is with the waveform view available.

In the waveform view, it's easy to trim off either end to eliminate unwanted data, or even to remove data from anywhere within the waveform. If the recording went on for a few seconds too long, it's very

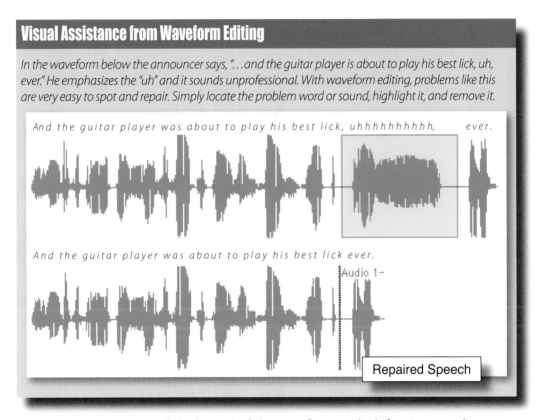

Visual Assistance from Waveform Editing

In the waveform below the announcer says, "…and the guitar player is about to play his best lick, uh, ever." He emphasizes the "uh" and it sounds unprofessional. With waveform editing, problems like this are very easy to spot and repair. Simply locate the problem word or sound, highlight it, and remove it.

And the guitar player was about to play his best lick, uhhhhhhhhhh,   ever.

And the guitar player was about to play his best lick ever.

Audio 1–

Repaired Speech

easy to slide the end of the waveform to the left, trimming the excess. Only the portion of the wave that's seen is heard.

Punch-In

The punch-in, when using a hard disk recorder, holds a different level of intensity and precision than when using a tape-based recorder. In the tape-based domain, the punch-in is destructive—one mistake and an entire phrase might be ruined.

There is an art to tape-based punch-ins. The operator learns to punch in and out of record with amazing precision. Replacing a word or portion of a word is common. However, one slip of the finger, one note held a little too long by the performer, and the material before, during, and after the intended record zone is damaged, usually irreparably.

With the advent of computer-based recording, the art form of punching in and out of record is dying. No longer do the recordist and the artist need to work perfectly together in the same "zone" to perform the perfect series of punches repeatedly. Most computer-based systems offer a "fast punch" option, but if you happen to make a mistake, it's no big deal. Simply access the waveform edit window and resize the audio boxes to include whatever you need from the old and new takes. Even if it sounds like you cut off part of the original audio, it can be easily resurrected and positioned to perfection. No problem!

Fixing the Digital Punch-In

Even though the punch-in, circled on B, looks like it erases over some of the good part of the take, all is well because the data still exists. Simply grab the end of the waveform blocks to close in or open up the waveform blocks. Once the edit point in B is moved to the right on the new lyric, the original good take can be opened back up to include the portion that appeared to be erased. Digital editing like this provides ample freedom to experiment without the fear of ruining anything. Even when it looks like damage is done, it probably isn't.

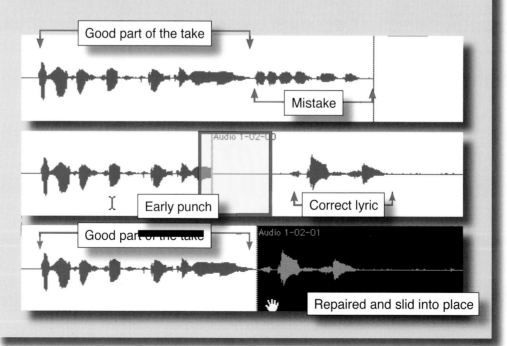

And while you're at it, if the performance was a little ahead of or behind the groove, just move it around in time until it feels great. Then, if it was a little out of tune, just shift the pitch until it's perfectly in tune. With all these tools available to perfect your music, you can concentrate on the important details, like "double pepperoni, double cheese" or "the veggie special" or Subway or Blimpie.

Auto Record

The auto record feature has been in use for a while in the analog domain—especially in the video and film realms. It provides a means to let the device shift into and out of record mode automatically, in reference to user-prescribed time code locations. This is particularly useful for the solo artist/technician/recordist. Punching in and out while playing an instrument is very difficult without auto record.

Auto record is also very convenient in the video and film domain. If a music or ambience change is required at a very specific point, simply program the auto record to punch in and out at the perfect SMPTE points.

Channels, Tracks, and Takes

A few terms are often used interchangeably, although they refer to different interrelated functions. Tracks, channels, and takes are not all the same. These words need to be differentiated so the concepts can be understood and put into practice.

Channels reside on a mixer. Each of the identical rows of faders, knobs, and buttons is a channel. To say a system has 24 channels refers only to the mixer, not to the multitrack recording capabilities.

Tracks are individual recording zones on a multitrack recorder. A 24-track analog tape recorder has 24 separate portions spread evenly across the width of tape. Audio is recorded separately across the horizontal distance of the tape. A modular digital multitrack operates on the same horizontal track scheme.

The computer-based digital recorder also has *tracks*. Although there's no tape, a track is still represented on a list, and the onscreen transport operates along a horizontal line like the tape-based systems.

A track in a digital system typically has provisions for its own level, balance, equalization, and routing control (its own channel) within the software realm, just as it would in a traditional analog setup.

Takes add another dimension to tracks. When a track is created and the instrument is recorded, you're done—in the tape-based domain. The computer setup, on the other hand, provides for multiple takes on each track. Without creating another track, a completely separate take can be recorded. In this way, the track list remains small and manageable, while the possibilities for creating options for each track are virtually limitless—depending on available disk space.

There are many applications for the concept of multiple takes. Takes are particularly convenient on lead vocal tracks, as well as instrumental solo and fill tracks. Most software packages that combine MIDI and digital audio allow for multiple takes on all tracks, no matter which type.

Comping

Comping is a technique that has been used in the multitrack world for about as long as it has been in existence. The concept is simple—find the best parts from several takes, then compile them into one track that represents the performance in the very best way.

This is a technique commonly used on lead vocals. Since they convey much of the meaning and emotion of a song, the lead vocals should be flawless if possible: flawless in emotion, rhythm, pitch, sound quality, and impact.

If vocalists could just sing for 16 hours straight with no break, if they'd sing every note perfectly in tune, if they were always rhythmically in the pocket, and if they could keep their energy and emotional fire intact for the duration, their tracks would be simple—and there would be no need for comping. Realistically, there is a point of no return for most vocalists—a point where their voice and attitude get worse instead of better. There is an art to recording lead vocals, and it requires constant motivation and positive reinforcement on your part. A good producer knows how to keep a singer in the game.

Most vocalists work best when they know they've got at least one track as a backup—a track that's been recorded and is good enough to use in case nothing better comes out. This reassurance is usually enough to loosen the singer up, and sure enough, the forthcoming takes are more relaxed and creative. A vocalist typically needs to take some chances to get the performance to the next level.

Once you've recorded a good take, record another take but save the old version. The computer-based system allows for plenty of takes, so let the singer fly a bit. Record several takes straight through the song. Stop as seldom as possible. Only stop to focus on a section that you know hasn't quite made it to the perfection of the previous takes. When you have several takes and you're convinced that somewhere in the file, each section has been performed to the highest standards, you've succeeded.

The actual comping process involves reevaluating each take. Use a lyric sheet to mark the best take for each lyric. Once you're convinced you know where each chunk of brilliance is located, start compiling all the sections to one new track. Simply copy from the source takes, then paste to the new comped track.

For each part, record each performance as a separate take on one track. Then, when it's time to comp, create a new track below the original performance track. Copy each desired section, then drag it down to the comped track—preferably locked to a time grid so as to remain in the same groove reference. This technique helps keep the confusion level to a minimum, both onscreen and in your head.

Once all the preferred sections are in place, some adjustments to edit points, level, equalization, or pitch might be necessary. There's usually a way to get the comped track to sound smooth and natural, as if it was the

Comping the Lead Vocal

It's common to record several versions of a track for review at a later date. Comping is the art of compiling portions from various takes in a way that sounds like one excellent take. When performed with skill, this procedure is transparent—it sounds like the tracks were always meant to be the way they end up. Comping vocal tracks lets the artist keep the best of each take. It also provides a system that lifts a little pressure off singers. They don't have to perform a flawless take. They don't have to second guess whether they can do a better complete performance. Neither do they have to continually experience vocal fatigue from countless tries at a complete performance. Comping is time consuming, but it results in incredible-sounding vocal tracks.

TAKE 1	The prince and the poet found romance in South Hampton.
TAKE 2	The prince and the poet found romance in South Hampton.
TAKE 3	The prince and the poet found romance in South Hampton.
TAKE 4	The prince and the poet found romance in South Hampton.
TAKE 5	The prince and the poet found romance in South Hampton.
COMP	The prince and the poet found romance in South Hampton.

only take of the day, but sometimes it requires some effort. Crossfading between regions serves to smooth out many rough spots.

If an edit isn't sounding smooth and you've exhausted your available technology and patience, go back the source takes to look for more options. Sometimes this process takes a while; an amazing lead vocal gives the music its greatest chance of success.

Tuning

A great-sounding recording that was made prior to the technological boon we're in commands much respect. There are musical problems that we almost routinely repair and perfect today; our predecessors would have toiled for hours to achieve similar results. We take for granted the minute control available to each of us regarding intonation, timing, and all the mix parameters.

Intonation is definitely an attribute that we, as modern recordists, can effectively manipulate. If a note is a little out of tune, we don't need to ruin the singer trying to get it a little closer. We can simply tune it.

With the auto-tune software packages available now, it's not even necessary to have a good ear or perfect pitch to ensure that all vocals or instruments are in tune. Simply set the parameters within the software package and process the desired audio; your part will be tuned to your specified perfection. Auto-Tune by Antares provides 19 different scales to reference intonation, along with the facility for graphical interface, vibrato (leaving it alone and creating it), and tolerance settings. Mackie offers an auto-tune plug-in for their D8B Digital Mixer that's also very impressive—and it's right in the console.

Audio Example 3-12

Out of Tune Vocal

Automatic Tuning

Automatic tuning programs offer digital pitch analysis and repair. In the time it takes the player or singer to perform with inaccurate intonation, the processor can analyze the pitch, guess where the tonal center should have been, and repair the problem. This all happens in real time. The specific scale type can be indicated as well as the type and degree of vibrato included or created.

Audio Example 3-13

Automatic Vocal Retuning

With the depth of technology available today, it's possible to tune a song too much. Stylistically, certain notes and inflections should be slightly out of tune. The "blue" note, for example, often works its way from just above one pitch to just below the next; it's never quite in tune with any one note in our tempered tuning scheme. Since much popular music is based on blues in some way, there are many instances where perfect intonation is simply inappropriate.

Depending on the style and accuracy of the vocalist, I often prefer to tune vocal parts by ear. Great singers working together can create a powerful impact. Much of their natural intonation is driven by emotional and musical tendencies. It's often best to capture a great performance, then tweak as little as possible to get the right feeling for the song. Sometimes very few changes are required; sometimes an amazing change must be made. Everything depends on musical considerations.

Finding the Groove

Shifting tracks in time is a feature unique to the digital era. In the analog, tape-based domain, a singer or instrumentalist is required to control the performance relative to the groove. In the digital domain, though ideally the musician will produce the very best possible performance, if a portion is a bit out of the pocket (not in time) it can be easily slid into place.

When vocals are recorded along with a MIDI sequence, finding the groove becomes extremely easy. The MIDI beat grid is typically right there onscreen. With graphic waveforms built along with the sequence, the beginnings of notes and words are simple to spot at a given location. Slide the audio waveform back and forth until the feel is right.

With controls like these available, it becomes increasingly important that the recordist have musical skills, understanding, and opinions. A technical engineer with no basis for making musical judgement calls must rely on the expertise of a skilled and experienced musician to effectively use the features and flexibility available in today's musical tools.

Listen to Audio Example 3-14 and notice the hyperactive feel of the guitar part.

Audio Example 3-14

Hyper-Sounding Guitar Part

Now listen to the same guitar part used in Audio Example 3-14, this time with the guitar shifted backward in time. This type of change is simple and instantaneous. Producing the same results in the analog domain would require a lot of time and at least one generation loss in quality. Digital manipulations like this produce absolutely no loss in audio integrity and require insignificant amounts of time and energy.

Audio Example 3-15

Repaired Guitar Groove

Quantizing Audio Segments

Though quantizing is known primarily as a MIDI function that is capable of conforming MIDI notes and data to a specified time grid, this capability is also applicable to audio segments within combined audio/MIDI software packages.

Since, as a rule, the beginning points of digital audio segments aren't consistent, quantizing audio isn't a common function. However, when building a percussive instrumental track from many repeated segments that have been carefully trimmed, audio quantizing is very usable. Like MIDI data, audio segments can be quantized to varying amounts, degrees, and percentages of user-defined note values.

Listen to Audio Example 3-16. It uses voice and percussive natural sounds to create a rhythmic groove. The individual ingredients were laid into the edit window so they were close to their intended beats, but little attention was paid to precision.

Next, listen to Audio Example 3-17. The audio segments have been quantized to the closest sixteenth note at 85 percent strength. The effect of this quantizing technique is dramatic.

Audio Example 3-16

Percussive Sounds with Loose Groove

Audio Example 3-17

Percussive Sounds with Quantized Groove

Moving Audio Segments

There are some basic ways to move audio segments. The specifics depend on the software you use, but most packages offer some version of each of these features.

Spot Mode

Spot mode lets the user enter a specific start or end time for the audio segment. For example, entering a start point of 01:01:00:00 places the selected region on the timeline so it begins at that SMPTE time.

This feature is very useful in the film and video realm. The sound designer's video work copy contains an onscreen time code window with scrolling SMPTE, which displays the correct time code throughout the program. If you've recorded a sound effect of an egg hitting the ground, which needs to be added at the precise time the egg begins to splat, the procedure is simple if you use spot mode. Simply roll the video, frame by frame, to the splat point. Then, type that SMPTE time into the start time window with the egg splat sound selected, and it's placed precisely where it should be—no trial and error, no guesswork.

For length-specific programming, like radio and television programs, end spotting is an important feature. If you need the last bit of reverb to trail out at 59 seconds, simply enter 00:00:59:00 in the end time window. This type of spotting, called *back placing*, is commonly used in the broadcast field.

Slip Mode

Slip mode lets the user slide an audio region smoothly along the timeline. This is a wonderful mode when adjusting timing. If the drummer was pushing the groove all the way through the song, simply select the entire track. Then, zoom the view in as far as possible so that you can see the smallest of time shifts. Then, manually slide the track back a

Spot Mode

Spot mode is the most convenient way to place audio segments at just the right spot. Simply enter the exact time position for either the beginning or end of the segment, and it shows up perfectly positioned. For film and video sound design, there's no better mode. Watch the work copy for the time code reference of a sound effect, and spot it in place.

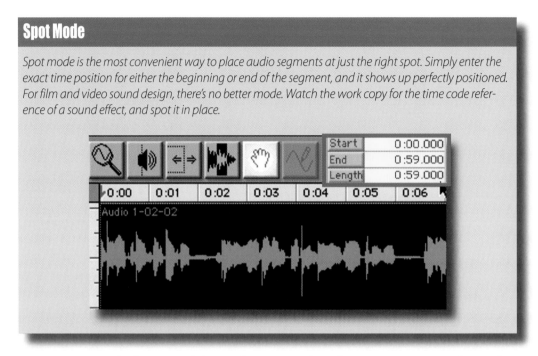

little in time. This might require a bit of experimentation and time, but the effort is well worth it when the groove tightens up.

As previously discussed, the same procedure works well on any track. Vocals and instrumental solos especially benefit from the availability of this feature.

Slip mode is also a very convenient way to rough in dialogue, music, and sound effects for slide presentations, radio programs, and documentaries.

Grid Mode

Grid mode is similar to slip mode in that audio regions can be slid along the timeline. It differs from slip mode in that, instead of sliding smoothly, the regions click along a user-selected grid. If the grid is set to quarter notes, regions will only stop on beat one, two, three, or four.

This mode is especially useful when developing rhythmic patterns with audio regions.

Shuffle Mode

Shuffle mode forces regions to butt together; it's particularly useful in speech editing. If a word or phrase is cut, instead of a space remaining where the phrase was, the phrase following the cut snaps over next to the phrase before the cut.

This mode is also very useful in song editing, where entire sections are removed. With this type of editing, it's necessary to bring the remaining regions together, so this automatic shuffling is very convenient.

Multitrack Backing Vocals

Backing vocals are very important to a song's impact. If they're done well, they can help the song convey its message in a stronger way. If they're performed, recorded, and edited poorly, they become a distraction and indicate a shabby project.

Tightening the performance during recording helps save time in the editing process and helps keep the quality standards high. Even when the vocals are very clean and tight, there are still several places the editor can help. Breaths, entrances, releases, and intonation are all factors that must be perfected to facilitate a professional-sounding product.

It's very common to double and triple backing vocals. For the following considerations, we'll assume all parts have been at least doubled. When a group sings tracks together, these factors should be addressed during the performance, since they're sometimes difficult to cover up during mixing. If the vocal group or individual sings with energy, life, and precision during tracking, the recordist should be able to quickly tighten any loose ends to create an impressive sound.

Breaths

The worst thing to do on any vocal track is to take out all breaths. For a track to sound natural, real, and believable, some breaths need to be heard; they make the recording sound alive. However, they shouldn't be so loud that they're distracting to the lead vocals or to the instrumental bed.

With a digital editor, breaths during backing vocals can easily be turned down, left out, or repositioned. The most important consideration is the groove. If the breaths are left in as part of the track's life, they need to be in time with the groove. If they're not, move them, turn them down, or eliminate them. Musical judgement is the key.

Listen to Audio Example 3-18. Notice how the breaths are out of time and a little too loud.

Audio Example 3-18
Breaths Out of Time

Next, listen to Audio Example 3-19. Notice how the breaths have been shifted in time and adjusted slightly in volume. Now they maintain life but add to the rhythmic feel of the arrangement.

Audio Example 3-19
Breaths Placed Rhythmically Correct

Entrances

One of the primary indicators of well-sung, cleanly performed backing vocals is the precision of the entrances. If every part starts together, they'll probably stay together, often all the way through the release.

Entrances are easy to place. It's always clear where the waveform begins and, when the backing vocal tracks are lined up vertically, any part that's slightly out of time is instantly detectable. The computer-based digital recording system is laid out perfectly for fine-tuning these details. The illustration below demonstrates how easy it is to see when tracks are out of the groove. It also shows the same tracks after the vocals have been slid into place to produce a precise vocal performance.

Audio Example 3-20 demonstrates the sound of a backing vocal with sloppy entrances.

Cleaning Up Sloppy Entrances

Notice how the backing vocals (A, B, and C) don't line up perfectly with the lead vocal at the vertical line. In the analog domain, this scenario is difficult and time consuming to correct. In the computer-based digital domain, repairing this problem is as easy as clicking on the waveform and sliding it into perfect rhythmic alignment.

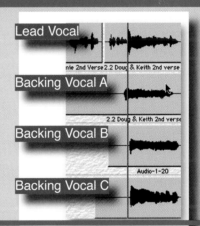

These are the same vocal parts again; however, they've been slid into position so all backing vocal tracks (A, B, and C) line up rhythmically with the lead vocal. Now all parts work together as a unit and the sound is impressive and powerful. It's always ideal to get the vocal parts as close to perfect as possible during tracking. However, if the singers are having a difficult time and the session is growing long, this technique can be a life saver. Fixes like this not only help tighten the arrangement, but they also help facilitate momentum through the song.

Sloppy Vocal Entrances

Listen to Audio Example 3-21 to hear the same piece of music with all entrances clean and precise.

Cleaned-Up Vocal Entrances

Releases

Releases are nearly as important as entrances to the polished feel of a song. The most critical releases are *transient releases*. Words that end in s, t, k, sh, and ch sounds are very distracting when the tracks lack precision.

With a digital editor and some patience, these ending sounds can be easily lined up with great precision after the fact. As with breath placement, these sounds should fit together nicely with the groove. Transients act like additional percussion instruments in most cases, so they should be placed with that in mind.

Audio Example 3-22 has some sloppy releases that distract from the groove.

Sloppy Releases

Listen to Audio Example 3-23 to hear how much better the backing vocals sound when they're working together on the releases.

Cleaned-Up Releases

Cleaning Up Sloppy Releases

Precise releases are an important ingredient in a well-sung arrangement. In a computer-based system sloppy releases are easy to slide into place. Depending on how rhythmically consistent the entire phrase is, some cutting and sliding might be needed to keep the groove constant throughout the phrase. Additionally, with modern recording software, time expansion and compression are easy to accomplish, providing a powerful tool for tightening up tracks.

With the releases tightened up, not only does the entire phrase sound better, but the phrase that follows has the opportunity for greater impact if it's precise. Notice how audio segments A, B, and C finish together.

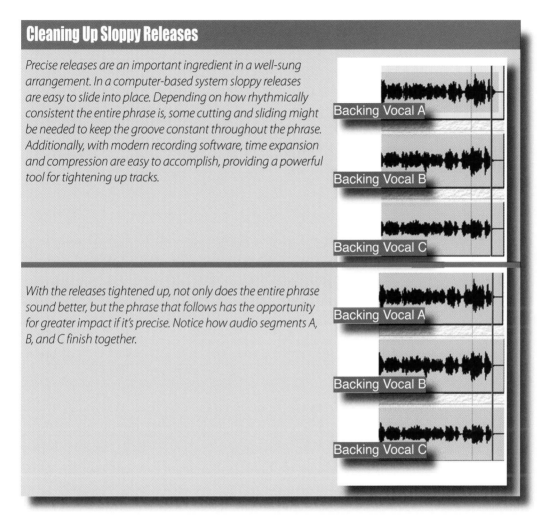

Intonation

Tuning is very important to the impact and professionalism of the recorded sound. As indicated earlier in this chapter, it's unrealistic to expect a work to command respect in the music community if care hasn't been taken to ensure appropriately precise intonation.

One of the problems in backing vocals is fading intonation over the course of a long note. Since the vocalists are often singing along with themselves or others, it's easy for them to lose track of pitch as they hold long notes—so they go flat or sharp.

This problem can be dealt with manually by retuning just a portion of the note and burying the edit point in the mix; some software packages also address this problem. For example, the now defunct Opcode developed a clever feature called Audio-to-MIDI, which analyzed the audio data and created MIDI parameters to correspond to note value, velocity, volume, tone, and pitch bend. With this technology, it was possible, once the MIDI parameters have been created, to adjust any parameter as if the audio had always been MIDI data.

With this process, if a note slides flat, then sharp, then flat again, that movement is registered as pitch bend data. The recordist can simply redraw the pitch bend data as a straight line at zero, therefore eliminating any variance in pitch. Next, the edited audio could be recreated through the MIDI-to-Audio command and the vocal track would play back with perfectly consistent intonation. Antares Auto-Tune plug-in provides this type of control in their Graphical made.

Detuning

In the digital domain, it's a simple task to detune an entire track. In the analog domain, detuning between tracks to create a bigger vocal sound could be accomplished by slighty varying the tape speed between takes—typical speed variations are between one and seven cents. Digitally, the same effect can be created in a nondestructive way. Raise or lower the pitch of one or more recorded vocal tracks, then blend the vocals together. If you don't like the sound, undo the action. Try another pitch change amount and blend again.

Listen to Audio Example 3-24 to hear a doubled backing vocal track, first as it was originally sung, then with the backing vocal tracks detuned by five cents.

Audio Example 3-24

Detuning the Vocal Track by Five Cents

Readjusting Formants

Detuning fattens because it changes the overtone structure of the vocal sound, simulating the effect of a different vocalist or group on the altered track. With modern digital editing packages, formants can be adjusted separately from pitch. Since formants control the apparent size of the voices, independent of the pitch, this adjustment can produce some amazing vocal effects. Alter the formant slightly on one of the backing vocal tracks for a fat sound.

Audio Example 3-25 demonstrates a tripled backing vocal track with the center as recorded, left with raised formants, and right with lowered formants.

Audio Example 3-25

Tripled Backing Vocal with Altered Formants

Fills, Frills, and Licks

The digital domain is wonderful for recording, moving, altering, and comping solos and licks. It's very convenient to just let the soloists play. Let them fill the track. Have them perform multiple takes—keeping them all, of course. Once you're sure you have enough to work with, thank 'em kindly and pay 'em highly. They'll be on their way, happy to receive your call another day, and you'll have lots of material to work with. It's better to have too much than too little.

Only select the necessary frills. It's anticlimactic to include too many hot licks. However, just the right amount provides a powerful musical addition. It's common to assemble solos and licks together from different takes or to use a lick that was originally performed at the end of a song in the early part of the song. With the incredible flexibility available in modern technology, you can make your decisions based on musical considerations rather than performance positioning.

Broadcast Audio

Voice-Over/Editing Speech

The digital editor is an incredibly powerful tool! We've been given control over almost every imaginable voice and music parameter. You can let your creativity run free in this medium. Musically, instrumentally, or in speech, you can usually produce anything you can imagine.

To alter a recording in a way that puts words in someone's mouth is child's play. Converting a public speech from a nervous and bumbling state to a slick and polished form is not difficult. The responsibility given to the editor is awesome. Listen to Audio Example 4-1.

Audio Example 4-1

Original Statement

Now listen to Audio Example 4-2. Notice how different the content is from Audio Example 4-1, even though it's simply an edited version of the same audio segment.

Application of Voice Editing

The advertising, radio, and television industries are built around speech. Narration, dialogue, and monologue are key forms of communication in these mediums. Dialogue replacement is commonplace in the world of film and video. An amazing number of movies utilize absolutely no field audio. Often, all speech, ambience, and sound effects are added in after the film has been edited. The world of multimedia uses speech as a common thread to hold the video, picture, and text together.

Speech editing is a huge part of the audio industry. Many engineers work their entire career without ever recording music. A voice editor who is both easy to be around and can perform high-quality work quickly and efficiently is a valuable commodity.

Voice-Over

The *voice-over* is simply a recording of one or more voices over a music, ambience, or sound effects bed. The person speaking the voice-over is referred to as the *talent*. Good voice talent is valuable. The ability to read the voice-over text (called *copy*) in a fluid, natural, and believable way is not an inherent gift, built into our species. In fact, inexperienced talent makes for an excruciating voice-over session. Excellent talent makes for a great day in the studio.

Even the most capable and experienced talent makes a mistake now and again. For the recordist, mistakes turn into edits.

Timing

One of the characteristics of prime talent is the ability to pace copy in the way that will be the most powerful. Delivery timing is fundamental to the voice-over's impact. Often, however, the talent must adjust the delivery timing simply to fit the copy within specified time constraints.

It's more likely that there will be too much copy for the allotted time than too little. The editor's challenge is to fit the copy in while maintaining a natural flow. Always leave at least a couple spaces where the listener could imagine talent taking a quick breath. Small breath spaces serve to punctuate the copy, drawing the listener in.

Eliminate unnatural pauses. Keep the flow moving ahead. Don't be afraid to tighten everything up so the copy has momentum. With only a small breath space or two, copy can flow quickly and still impact the listener.

Ambience

Voice-overs are usually very dynamically compressed, but they're typically recorded in a very quiet voice-over booth. This small recording room is designed to minimize reflections and to provide a warm, smooth speaking sound. Most professionally recorded voice-overs have no problem with ambience changes from take to take—their recording environment is designed to minimize ambient influence.

Field audio, however, is captured on location. Recording a speech in front of a crowd offers special challenges. The sound reinforcement system adds to the character of the voice, feedback can be an issue, crowd noises are always a consideration, and other background noise is often changing constantly. Smoothing together phrases or eliminating stammers and false starts is easy in the controlled environment of the studio because there's no ambience change. Audio from the field contains continual changes in ambience; the simplest of edits are often complicated by a sneeze or a baby's cry.

Problematic Edits

When confronted with problematic edits you have a few options that can serve very well to hide, obscure, or eliminate them. Try these features, one at a time, until you're satisfied that the edit is satisfactory.

Crossfade Ambience

With a little experimentation, crossfades can often smooth over an ambience change at an edit point. Adjust the crossfade length and shift the edit point until you find the right combination.

Music Bed

When the situation calls for a music bed under field audio, try positioning the music bed so it strategically swells or so that an instrument enters at the ambience change. Music adds cohesiveness to almost any speaking part. It also helps smooth over edits.

Add Ambience

If the edit point sounds too abrupt no matter what you do with music or crossfades, listen closely to the ambience change. Once you hear the sound of the loudest ambience, try to find a portion of the recording that has that ambient sound alone. When the proper ambience is located, copy a few seconds, then paste it onto another track at the same point as the edit in question. Fade the ambience up and then down at the edit point. This technique is very effective in most cases.

Audio Example 4-3

Adding Ambience to Match Takes

Reconstruct the Scene

Film and video sound present these ambience change problems all the time. If a line simply must be heard and understood but there's a distraction like a huge truck rumbling in the background over the first half of it, you might need to rerecord the line. Try reconstructing the scene. Either go back on location to record the questionable portion in a cleaner ambient environment, or assess the ambient sound and recreate the recording electronically. It's amazing how well a field voice texture can be replicated in the studio. Try to equalize the sound to match. If possible, use the same mic setup that was used in the field. If the field

Adding Ambience to Match Takes

Often, separate parts of a dialogue are recorded in different places and at different times. Ambience changes between recordings can be distracting and annoying. It's good procedure to record a few minutes of silence each time you record voice. This silence, called room tone, can be used to feather ambiences together. In the graphic below, differing ambiences are represented by changes in shading. If we've recorded some gray ambience, it's simple to use a digital editing system to lay it in under the white ambience track to provide a constant room feel. Version A plus additional ambience A (version B) produces constant ambience (version C).

Voice A	Voice B	Voice A	Voice B
Ambience A	Ambience B	Ambience A	Ambience B
The music police entered the room.	What did they say?	They said, "Stop! You're busted! Don't ever play that skanky country lick in a heavy metal song again. You have the right to remain silent!"	What did you do?

Version A

Voice A	Voice B	Voice A	Voice B
Ambience A	Ambience B	Ambience A	Ambience B
The music police entered the room.	What did they say?	They said, "Stop! You're busted! Don't ever play that skanky country lick in a heavy metal song again. You have the right to remain silent!"	What did you do?
	Sampled Ambience A		Sampled Ambience A

Version B

Voice A	Voice B	Voice A	Voice B
Ambience A	Ambience A	Ambience A	Ambience A
The music police entered the room.	What did they say?	They said, "Stop! You're busted! Don't ever play that skanky country lick in a heavy metal song again. You have the right to remain silent!"	What did you do?

Version C

audio had some natural reverberation, try to simulate it digitally. As the final ingredient, copy some field ambience from the original recording. Place it on another track at the insert point and use it to bridge the gap between the real audio and the reconstructed audio.

Live with It

If the nature of the program material is primarily informational, it might be appropriate to just accept the abrupt edit. All good editors try to do the very best job possible, but there are applications where an obvious edit isn't the end of the world. Judgement calls are the norm in the day-to-day world of audio production. Sometimes the details are in control; other times the deadline is in control.

Breaths

Speech is often very compressed to keep each syllable at the forefront of the mix. The drawback, technically, to this approach is that along with every word that's enhanced by the compressor's level adjustments comes every breath, lip smack, sniff, and tongue clack. In many applications, these distracting sounds must be diminished or removed. Notice in Audio Example 4-4 how pronounced the breaths and mouth sounds are.

Audio Example 4-4

Pronounced Breath and Mouth Sounds

Some breaths and mouth sounds should simply be eliminated. Other sounds just require a gain adjustment. If you remove all breaths, your recording will lack life, authenticity, and believability. Practice various techniques and approaches until you have a feel for what it takes to produce a real-sounding voice edit.

Pronounced Breath and Mouth Sounds

It's best to deal with these sounds before they hit the air waves (radio or television). If they're irritating on the master, they'll be even more pronounced after the broadcast compressors have emphasized them further. Either cut the breaths altogether or use the virtual mixer to turn the track down quickly during the breath and back up for the voice.

Simply cutting the breath out typically only works well when the voice is over a bed of music—there needs to be some background sound to mask the change in ambience as the voice track cuts in and out. If you must cut the breath completely, add some ambience from another portion of the same voice recording to help fill in the gap, much like the previous illustration.

The blue line running through the wave represents the volume control that you typically find in recording software packages. Notice how it dips down at the breaths and lip smack. This is a much smoother way to solve vocal noise problems than simply cutting them.

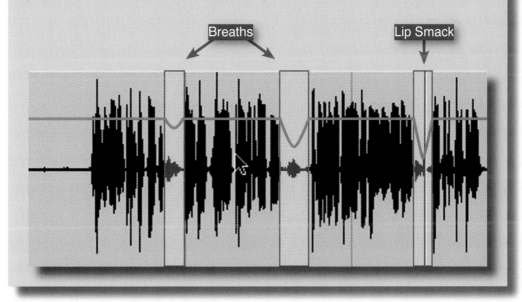

Now listen to Audio Example 4-5. Notice how much more impact the text has with the distracting breaths and mouth sounds turned down or eliminated.

Audio Example 4-5

Repaired Breath and Mouth Sounds

Time Compression/Expansion

Time compression and expansion are used commonly in the broadcast world. A 30-second commercial needs to end in between 29 and 30 seconds. If a spot is short and runs at 26 or 28 seconds, it not only messes up the programming, it's an inefficient use of airtime. Total production cost for an ad is typically several thousand dollars, so the motivation is to use every valuable second.

Voice recordings can usually be compressed or expanded by 10 to 15 percent with little adverse effect on the impact of the text. Whenever time-adjusting audio, act primarily on the voice. When speech is altered and the music is left in its original state, the results are more consistently satisfying.

Listen to Audio Examples 4-6 through 4-10. The voice has been time-adjusted by varying percentages, which are indicated in the recording. Notice the character of the voice at each degree of compression or expansion.

Audio Example 4-6
Original Voice-Over

Audio Example 4-7
Voice-Over Expanded by 10 Percent

Audio Example 4-8
Voice-Over Expanded by 20 Percent

Audio Example 4-9
Voice-Over Compressed by 10 Percent

Audio Example 4-10
Voice-Over Compressed by 20 Percent

ADR/Foley

ADR and *Foley* are two terms commonly used in the film and television worlds:

+ ADR stands for *automatic dialogue replacement.* The process involves rerecording dialogue that's already been filmed or videotaped.

+ A Foley soundstage is designed to support the replacement of natural sounds like footsteps, door slams, and creaks and other things that stomp, squeak, thump, or bump.

ADR

The need for ADR arises from three primary factors: poorly recorded field audio, a desire to project more intimacy with the character than the ambient field audio allows, and line changes.

Capturing high-quality field audio is an art. It's difficult to capture the intimacy of a scene from outside the camera view; sometimes it's impossible. When the field audio is not effective for the scene, the actors are required to come to the studio. In this controlled environment, an intimate sound is easy to capture. The process involves actors watching themselves on a video monitor while they re-speak the dialogue. Each actor tries to recreate the correct inflections, pacing, and emotion for the scene.

This is sometimes a tedious process, but it's amazing how convincing the rerecorded audio is. It's also amazing how many movies use ADR for all spoken parts. Next time you watch a movie, try to imagine whether the ambient sound of the voice matches the indicated ambience of the setting.

It's common that the film producer or director wants the audience to feel like they're intimate with the actors in a given scene. Therefore, no matter what the surrounding ambience or quality of field audio, ADR is needed.

Any film recordist deals constantly with text rewrites. At the last minute, an important line in the film might be changed. Line changes seldom involve reshooting the video or film because of budgetary reasons, but they often involve ADR and some creative scene editing. An attempt is made to obscure the actor's mouth during a scene with a line change. A distant, side, or rear shot might be selected. However, often the production staff decides to rely on the audience's inattention to detail. Watch movies with an alert eye. You'll see many scenes where the actors are saying something different than it looks like they're saying. This is a judgement call. The production team must decide if the line change is strong enough to warrant a visual discrepancy that most people will never notice.

ADR is typically done in reference to SMPTE time code. A scrolling image of the correct SMPTE time code is burned onto a video tape reference. With the digital editor locked to time code, the actors' lines are rerecorded as they try to match the picture. The reference videotape often includes the field audio for an audible reference, too.

Once the dialogue has been rerecorded and is very close to matching, the digital editor takes over. It's simple to slide the new audio into place. The nudge keys are very convenient. Simply select the nudge resolution that seems right for the job and slide the audio into place. It's best to use the nudge feature once the new audio is closely positioned because it gives the operator a frame of reference. If the audio is moved six nudges early but then seems a little too early, it's easy to guess that it might need to be moved back two or three nudges. If the audio is simply slid around, there's no frame of reference, and the task will take longer than it should.

Foley

The process for Foley recording is similar to that for ADR. Someone on the Foley soundstage watches a videotape of the program, trying to match the steps, slams, or squeaks with those onscreen. With waveform graphics and onscreen SMPTE time code available, placing most Foley sounds is a simple task. At the contact of the shoe with the ground, for example, you can note the time code reference and spot the rerecorded footstep perfectly in place. Most Foley sound effects can be easily positioned this way.

In the major film and video markets around the world, there are several highly skilled Foley artists who are very accurate in their placement of sounds. If you hire excellent Foley talent with an impressive arsenal of sound-creating gadgets, this process will go very smoothly, and you might not need to do much shifting or nudging at all.

Getting the Program Ready for the Air

Normalize

Once the voice is recorded and positioned, whether in radio, television, or film, it needs to be readied for presentation. First, be sure the levels of the audio are strong and full. If the track needs to be normalized, now is the time. Be sure that, if there are several edits within the voice-over, the entire track is normalized as one item. This mode looks for the peak across the entire track, then moves all levels up relative to the peak. Another mode normalizes each item separately. This is the wrong mode for normalizing a complete voice-over.

In music creation the purist holds a certain disdain for the normalizing process. It technically holds the potential of giving the audio a grainy sound if the levels are insufficient. Always strive to keep strong digital levels without overloading and realize that your broadcast audio must be strong and clean to sound good on air.

Normalizing by Region

When normalizing by region, the processor has no real way of telling which regions should be adjusted differently. It simply takes each region and normalizes it to the set specification—usually 100 percent level at the peak. When normalizing edited dialogue it's best to normalize the entire file as one event, then save it as a continuous file.

Especially in sections like the one marked below, normalizing by region results in artificially loud sections. Regions meant to be heard at low levels get boosted to full amplitude. Notice the difference in the original edit and the edit normalized by region—especially in the yellow-shaded area. This area that should be nearly silent ends up at full digital level. This does not produce a smooth-sounding voice track.

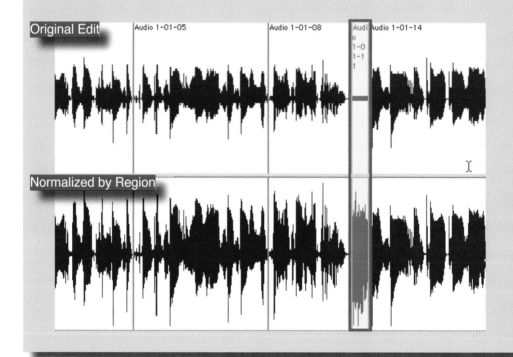

In the previous illustration you see a voice-over normalized two ways: one way as an entire track and the other as individual regions. Notice the dramatic difference in level between regions.

Audio Example 4-11

Edited Voice

Audio Example 4-12

Edited Voice Normalized by Region

Compression

If the voice-over track has a substantial difference between the loudest and softest portions, compress the entire track for the most natural, though consistently present, voice sound. It's very important to keep the voice level strong and in the front of the mix.

Compression is a standard part of most digital recording software packages. Some utilize a preview mode; with these, you must select the preview region according to its overall representation of the level extremes throughout the track. There will usually be an option to replace the original track completely or to simply add the new, processed track to the list. Keep the original track available as a safety.

Music

Usually music needs to be feathered in throughout a program to add to the flow and emotion of the presentation. Match the music level and the voice level so they both sound strong when they're alone. Because certain sounds appear to be louder than others, even at the same level, use your ears as well as your meters to predict how well your soundtrack will project.

Adjust the volume of accompanying music so that it is well below that of the voice. Always guess low on the music level; it should be under the voice-over level. A couple of things happen in the broadcast process that affect the final balance between the music and voice:

1. Multiband compression is used on most broadcast transmissions. A multiband compressor divides the audible spectrum into discrete ranges. Most broadcast compressors divide the transmission bandwidth into two or three frequency ranges: typically highs, mids, and lows. Each of these bands is compressed separately. The advantage to this process is that the bass, which contains the most energy of any frequency range, doesn't always hit the main threshold. Therefore, the bass doesn't continually cause the entire program to turn down. The drawback to this process is that the balance of the music and voice doesn't remain constant. Since the voice should be the strongest signal in its frequency range, it's constantly activating the compressor, causing it to turn its range down. If the bass range and treble range compress to a lesser degree, they probably increase in relation to the mids—the prime vocal range.

2. Limited bandwidth in the radio and television domain can cause a discrepancy between what is heard in the studio and what is heard on air. It's for this reason that recordists who work with broadcast often use a speaker or speakers designed to reproduce the sound of AM radio or mono television. To verify a program's viability in a broadcast medium, monitor through a multiband compressor and small, inexpensive speakers.

5

Digital Recording Hardware

Alesis started a recording revolution when it introduced the original ADAT. The eight-track digital recorder did so much for the money that it was irresistible to the entire industry. In addition to offering high-quality digital multitrack capability, the ADAT protocol allowed multiple machines to be synchronized together—hence the tag *modular digital multitracks*. In fact, they synchronized together with far greater accuracy than the best analog machines connected to the best machine synchronizers. Up to 16 ADATs could be daisy-chained together with near sample-accurate sync, for a whopping 128 tracks. With this system, the user was given the freedom to start with one ADAT, adding more modules as needed and as business supported.

Almost immediately, it seemed that recording facilities of all sizes jumped on the ADAT bandwagon. The excitement created by this device was evident at its introduction at the 1992 Audio Engineering Society show. After schmoozing for a pass from the folks at the Alesis booth to stand in line, everyone waited in line for a couple hours just to see it work. The implementation of a system that bridged the gap between home and the full-blown professional facility made it possible for all of us to do some of our work at home and some at a commercial studio. The industry went through a little bit of trauma while everyone positioned themselves for the coming revolution. Big studio owners started to band together to fight the home studio, and home studio owners kept buying equipment that let them do top-quality work at home.

Once everything settled down, a good working relationship started to form between the serious pro studios and the serious home studios. It's true that some studios in the middle ground were stretched to maintain commercial viability, but the audio, audio for video, and multimedia markets simultaneously opened up. When studios of the late '80s and early '90s were competing for music- and band-related projects, they had no idea of the multimedia revolution that was about to begin. The mid- and late-'90s brought much more business for studios of all sizes. With the advent of the Internet, multimedia, CD-ROM, online audio, and guerilla video, the project base became diverse and plentiful for those willing to hound out some business.

As gear got less expensive, the quality got higher. Anyone at home could produce a professional product if they knew how to use their gear. The only problem with this era was that too many people had the tools to do top-quality work without first learning how to produce top-quality product. As things have settled down, more young recordists have built expertise. In addition, equipment manufacturers have gotten better at providing user-friendly equipment that automatically handles format, technical, and artistic details in a way that increases the quality level throughout the industry.

Now we look at a future in the audio industry that allows the recordist to flourish. Certain functions are best accomplished at home. Other functions can only be done at a large professional facility. The better the recordist gets at producing top-quality audio at home, the more likely he or she is to rise to the level where a big studio is needed for certain phases of a project. The modular digital multitrack has made an impact on the audio industry indeed.

With the advent of the ADAT, other manufacturers jumped into the arena with their version of this convenient and flexible format. Whereas the ADAT used the SVHS video format, which held about 40 minutes of eight-track audio, the Tascam DA-88 used the Hi 8 video format for storage. Tascam's system aimed toward the film and video industry by providing a system that would store up to two hours per tape. Whereas ADAT dominated the home recording industry, DA 88s held their own in the film-scoring world. Alesis, of course, answered the challenges of both of these with updated models with longer record times and additional professional features—maintaining the ADAT format.

Comparison of MDMs to Computer-Based Systems

In the long run, both the computer-based hard disk recorder and the MDM hold an important place in the history of recording. As drive capacities and processor speeds continue to break technical barriers, MDMs have become less predominant than they were at first. They're simply not as convenient as software-based systems and they really haven't kept up with the trends in high-definition audio. There have been devices created that try to double resolution by splitting mono data between two tracks and other similar schemes, but MDM madness has faded.

MDMs excel at simultaneous recordings of many tracks. The fact that up to 16 MDMs can link together virtually like one machine is still impressive. It still takes an impressive computer-based system to record 128 simultaneous audio tracks for 40 straight minutes, even at 20-bit, 48-kHz resolution.

Keep in mind that MDMs use a video transport system. The tape your audio lives on follows much the same path that the tape in your VCR follows. How does that make you feel? The reality is that all MDM manufacturers have addressed this issue, and their tape-handling systems have gotten faster and much more reliable. However, with two or more MDMs, it's a simple matter to create a backup copy of every track in your production—and I'd recommend it.

I make backups of my backups, no matter what format I'm operating in. In a hard disk system, I make daily archives of my file status to CD or DVD. In the scope of a project, the cost of the extra tape or discs used to back up a project is incidental, especially considering the cost of rerecording everything. This concept is not specific to digital systems. It's also common to back up analog multitrack tapes. When I mix and match formats, I'll make a work copy of the analog multitrack (typically, two-inch tape, 24-track) that provides the reference while recording all the digital tracks (MDM and/or hard disk systems). The better your projects are, the more they need to be protected. Backups are important to the recording process in general.

MDMs also provide an excellent way to archive your hard disk-based recordings. Since a 24-, 48-, or 64-track hard disk recording typically occupies more than 650 MB, the CD isn't an appropriate archive medium without a utility designed to split the data between disks. That concept isn't incredibly bothersome, but as soon as you split the data up, there's more risk of part of it corrupting or being ruined. There's comfort in archiving everything in its perfectly crafted sync to a format that remains in sync and is quick and easy to call back up later. Personally, I archive in both formats when presented with this scenario. Archive to MDM and the disc format du jour. With the advent of DVD and other high-capacity storage media, file size is less of an issue, but multiple-format backups are still prudent.

In regard to speed and ease of use, nothing effectively competes with the hard disk system. However, where the hard disk system falls short, the MDM systems excel, and vice versa. The recording era has changed; no longer do we simply buy the popular reel-to-reel analog eight-track and call it a day. Now, we carefully combine the best of all worlds to help in our creative and musical endeavors.

MDM systems were manufactured by Fostex, Sony, and others. However, operational characteristics and technical specifications tended to mirror the updated status of the Alesis ADAT and Tascam DA series. The audio industry embraced the ADAT format, and we've all benefited from its excellent and insightful design. The original "black-face" ADATs still perform well in many applications. The MDM, though a fading glimpse of history, and the folks at Alesis deserve our gratitude for changing the face of the music business.

Dedicated Digital Recording Systems

Dedicated digital recording systems typically use a proprietary operating system to operate a self-contained digital studio. Audio is usually recorded on an internal hard drive, and all record and playback controls are located on the unit. No other computer is required for operation.

These systems have some advantages:

+ They don't tie up a computer. If you use your computer for other musical functions or if you don't own a computer, this might be a good way to go.

+ They often offer a smoother operation because they're not sharing a processor with other applications and utilities. One of the disadvantages of the computer-based system is timing. Occasionally during playback or record, multiple applications place timing demands on the processor. This sometimes results in an awkward rhythmic feel that's inconsistent from one pass to the next.

- Everything in the system is optimized specifically for a digital audio application. This results in a smooth-running system that doesn't crash often.

These systems also have some disadvantages:

- They're typically not as easily expandable as the computer-based or MDM systems. They contain a certain number of tracks that are simple to synchronize to MTC or SMPTE, although they're not always designed for expandability.

- They can only be used for one function. With a computer-based system, you have the ability to record audio, mix audio, play back audio, do word processing, keep your financial records, write a book, etc.

- They aren't usually as easy to update as a computer-based system. Though they can typically receive software upgrades, hardware is another question. Adding tracks, modules, effects, plug-ins, and other hardware-related functionality is often impossible or cumbersome.

Samplers

Keyboard-based samplers are essentially dedicated digital recording systems with some limited record functionality, along with some optimized playback functionality. The original samplers offered very limited sample time. A few seconds were typically available to divide among individual mono samples, which were spread across the keyboard. Modern samplers are limited by disk space. When they're connected to a large, fast hard drive, they can provide hours of full-bandwidth stereo audio.

Excellent samplers are manufactured by Korg, Kurzweil, Roland, Yamaha, and others. These keyboard-based systems add depth and character to any setup. The sample libraries developed for each of these instruments are incredible. In addition, several manufacturers can play back nearly any instrument's sounds. Most systems eventually grow to the point where a good sampler is an essential ingredient.

Many digital effects processors offer varying degrees of sample recording, playback, and manipulation. Companies like Lexicon and TC Electronic offer amazing sampling functionality from their digital effects processors.

Digital samplers provide most of the controls available in the MIDI domain, along with control over most digital audio parameters.

Sampling Keyboard Functions

Sampling keyboards offer many of the same functions as any other synthesizer, plus some additional features unique to the digital recording arena:

+ **Polyphony** – Several samples played across the keyboard

+ **Variable sample rates** – 32 kHz, 44.1 kHz, 48 kHz, etc.

+ **Sample editing** – Truncation, forward and backward looping, bidirectional looping, cut, copy, paste, and undo

+ **Layering** – Two or more sounds occurring simultaneously from the same keyboard stroke

+ **Reverberation, chorusing, and other effects**

- **Equalization**

- **Pitch adjustment and correction**

- **Gain normalization** – The ability to adjust the overall track volume so the strongest peak is at full digital level

- **Volume smoothing**

- **Wave sample mixing, merging, and splicing**

- **Data inversion, reverse, replication, addition, and scaling**

Hardware Ingredients of a Software-Based System

When you're building a software-based system, there is often accompanying hardware that's necessary in addition to the computer. It is possible to create a very simple system, much like the all-in-one systems we discussed previously. There are several devices available that contain the A/D converters, audio signal path, and D/A converters for playback and mixing. Combine these mixers with a mic and a computer for a complete studio setup.

If you're putting together a system that will expand to include multiple devices, you'll need more ingredients. You'll need a word clock source, MIDI interface, digital audio interface, optional digital or analog mixer, optional additional hard drives, and optional mix recorder. The beauty of this type of system is its ability to expand to whatever size you need. The disadvantages of this system are complexity and cost. As manufacturers have addressed the needs of the home recordist, more and more devices are combining several features necessary to complete the home recording setup.

The Digital Audio Interface

The digital audio interface contains the A/D converters necessary to convert the analog signal into digital data. Not only is this device fundamental to the recording process, but the technical quality of the converters is very important to the sound of the recording. Many serious recordists include in their systems high-quality outboard A/D and D/A converters designed to provide the very best conversions in and out of the digital domain. The sonic difference in transparency and definition is often immediately discernible when you upgrade to an expensive, high-quality outboard converter—sometimes the difference is subtle. This is an excellent opportunity to use your ears. If you're thinking about increasing the quality of your recordings by including an outboard converter, listen first, then buy.

Most audio interfaces contain multiple analog and digital inputs and outputs. The quality of analog connections varies from simple, consumer-level, –10-dBV RCA connections, to fully professional balanced +4-dBm XLR or 1/4-inch TRS connections.

Some very common interfaces provide eight channels of analog—along with 24 channels of digital—input and output connections. In addition, they often include headphone outputs; SP/DIF, AES/EBU, and optical connections; and inputs and outputs for word clock and other sync connections.

Some interfaces even include some sort of MIDI interface, although it's typically a bit simplistic. There's almost always some type of software interface for these devices, which provides a convenient and very graphic means of determining routing, audio preferences, computer connections, word clock functions, and more. If your audio interface is fully supported by your audio recording software, it will be easy to jump from one to the other in the software domain to facilitate quick changes in communication and functional parameters.

Audio interfaces connect to your computer in the same way as other peripherals, via FireWire, USB, PCI, etc. The most powerful interfaces connect to a card inserted into a PCI slot inside the computer. These PCI cards contain additional processing architecture which adds speed and capacity to the recording system. The most convenient and inexpensive interfaces connect via FireWire or USB-2. These interfaces take advantage of the speed of these communication buses, providing hot-swappable plug-and-play tools.

Some of the FireWire interfaces even accept power from the FireWire bus, so no external power supply is necessary to run the device. This is extremely convenient when connecting to a laptop computer in a portable system—don't forget extra computer batteries.

There is one advantage to USB-2 connections. Often, FireWire audio interfaces work best when they are the only device on the FireWire bus. Even if your computer has multiple FireWire connections, there's a good chance that there's only one FireWire bus. Connecting the audio interface to the USB-2 bus leaves the FireWire bus available for external hard drives.

The USB-1 protocol is too slow for use with an audio interface. By modern standards, USB-1 is great for keyboards, mouses, PDA interfaces, and MIDI-only interfaces, but that's about it.

In summary, interfaces connecting through the PCI bus are the most powerful and stable; interfaces connecting through the FireWire or USB-2 bus are convenient and inexpensive. Each system is capable of high-quality audio—the big difference is in processing capacity.

Clock Source

Every digital system needs some form of word clock source. This clock can come from a simple digital output or from a dedicated digital word clock generator.

If you're using one digital device, such as an all-in-one recording system, it simply runs in reference to its own internal word clock. Even though you don't need to deal with it, it's still functioning, driving your digital system.

As soon as you connect multiple digital devices together, you must be aware of the digital connection and how the system works together in reference to one master word clock. It's advisable to incorporate a high-quality, very stable word clock hub that generates all types of word clocks along with video reference clock. It is, however, convenient that AES/EBU, SP/DIF, and optical formats contain clock information along with the audio data. In a simple system it is common procedure to direct the slave device to reference any of these incoming formats.

The Importance of a Stable Clock Source

If the digital clock isn't stable, some of the samples are off slightly. When this happens a phenomenon called *jitter* happens. Jitter can compound from device to device in a large system, causing cumulative problems.

Jitter isn't a dramatic effect that you would probably even notice on one listen. However, the effect of jitter is a confusion in timing in the flow of the digital clock. Since timing cues are what provide spatial placement imagery for our hearing and perception of audio, the result of randomizing or confusing this information is a reduction in stereo or surround positioning and imagery. If your recordings seem to have a narrow or smeared spatial image, you might be referencing an unstable clock source.

Simple Digital-to-Digital Connections

Most digital devices can see a digital input and follow its clock sample for sample. They communicate in a simple master-slave relationship. Typically, the master and slaves are determined via a user-adjusted setting. Set the master device, connect its digital output to the digital input on the slave device, and set the slave device to receive clock data from the master device. This setup is easy and efficient but it is the simplest of clock connections. In order for devices to function completely in this setup, there must be a time reference connection to coordinate the devices in relation to measures and beats or hours, minutes, and seconds.

Digital-to-Digital Connections

Any time digital devices work together in real time, they must be following the same digital word clock. For example, if you want to record from one device to the other or if you're playing back from your digital audio interface through a digital mixer and the devices are not running solidly together, the results aren't good. You might not even get signal from one device to the other, and if you do actually get sound, it will be full of static or, at best, riddled with clicks and pops.

The setting for most devices is found in the Preferences menu or in Hardware Settings, Receive Sync, Sync To, or some similar location. The options you might find for setting a slave device are Clock Source, Word Clock, External Clock, Clock Modes, Sample-Accurate Sync, etc. The device that runs as the master should be set to Internal in the Sync menu.

Even in the simplest digital connections involving only two devices, the master device plays normally; however, the slave device must be set to follow the word clock of the incoming digital signal. It won't work to simply let both devices run freely, like you would in any analog connection.

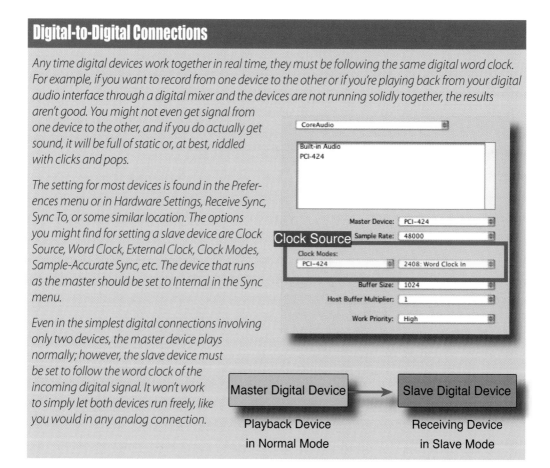

Dedicated Clock Source

If your system contains multiple digital devices working together, you must determine one device as the master word clock source for the entire system. It's important to incorporate a dedicated word clock device that has the capacity to output several types of clock data at once, so all system devices receive stable clock data and time reference. These devices provide timing information along with digital word clock generation, simultaneously generating SMPTE and MTC time codes.

When connecting a system with multiple digital devices, use high-quality sync cables. These connections must be solid and dependable. Most of the potential problems with a complex digital system have to do with poorly connected clock data.

When configuring your system, determine the master clock source, then follow the sync chain step by step, verifying the connection and configuration of each device in order, from master to the final slave. It's impossible to efficiently troubleshoot a digital clock problem if you don't verify each device in a very deliberate, calculated, and thorough manner.

Connecting Two Separate Systems

If you occasionally take your system to another studio, you might need to connect to their master word clock generator, often called *house sync*, in order to integrate with their digital system. This shouldn't be a problem as long as their system and yours are both stable. Simply connect the house sync to the word clock input on your master device. Next, set your device to slave to the incoming clock source. Ideally, your system will follow along without a problem.

If you experience difficulty functioning as a slave to the house sync generator, try slaving the studio clock to your clock generator. Almost all clock generators function in master or slave mode, and you might need to experiment to find which configuration works best in your situation. Some devices actually prefer to provide clock information rather than to receive it; some devices are rock-solid stable no matter how you connect them. These systems are sometimes easier to understand theoretically than they are to implement practically.

MIDI Interface

You must have an interface for connecting MIDI devices to your recording system. The MIDI interface provides several functions. It can

- Receive MIDI signals from keyboards, drum machines, and sound modules for delivery to the MIDI sequencing software.

- Receive data from the sequencer for delivery to the MIDI inputs for all connected MIDI devices.

- Send and receive MIDI timing information in the form of MIDI Time Code (MTC) for use in synchronization and time reference. Many devices contain loops, arpeggiation, or other time-dependent content that must follow the master time clock to remain in rhythmic sync. In addition, many digital mixer automation systems require MTC to reference automated parameter changes.

- Route MIDI connections between the computer, interface, and any connected MIDI devices.

- Filter data between connections. There are certain devices that don't need to receive all MIDI data. In fact, some devices don't function properly if they receive the wrong type of data or they simply receive too much data.

FireWire

The FireWire bus is overkill for a MIDI-only interface. Typically, interfaces that connect through FireWire contain digital audio, MIDI, and timing information. These systems are very convenient, fairly stable, and provide an efficient combination of protocols for your digital system.

USB

USB-1 connections are commonly used for MIDI-only connections, interfacing the computer-based recorder with a simple MIDI system. Often, the MIDI interface contains other capabilities, such as word clock generation and MIDI signal routing; it might even act as the clock source for your entire system. If this is the case, the USB-1 connection remains a MIDI-only connection, while the word clock connects via sync connections in the normal way. USB-1 doesn't carry digital word clock data, even though it does carry MIDI communication and timing data.

Serial

Serial connections are disappearing. They are slow relative to current and future demands in the audio recording realm. Though they function reasonably well in a MIDI-only system, they are very susceptible to MIDI data logjam problems.

Mixers

Digital

Your digital mixer must interface with the rest of your digital and analog gear in a way that is seamless and functional. Any digital device needs to communicate at the word clock level with all other digital devices in the setup. In addition, many digital mixers require MIDI in and out connections to send and receive timing information. This time reference is used in automation control and system integration. Also, MIDI connections can be used to send and receive MIDI control information to and from other system devices.

Many current digital mixers incorporate most of the necessary interface controls and capabilities. Mixers connecting through FireWire or USB-2 often contain the audio interface and the MIDI interface, along with all word clock and timing information. These systems are very convenient and easy to use.

Analog

If you're using your computer's internal audio capabilities or if you're incorporating a simple two- or four-channel soundcard, a small analog mixer connected to a couple powered monitors might be the perfect setup for you. Even though you might only need a very small mixer containing a couple channels for the outputs from your soundcard and one or two mic inputs to get the proper signal level into your computer, get the highest quality small mixer you can afford. It's important to accurately monitor the signals from your soundcard outputs and it's important that the mixer contain high-quality mic preamps that will accurately capture the sounds you record.

Mix Recorders

Historically, when we've discussed hardware included in any recording system, the mixdown recorder was a fundamental consideration. In this new era of technological advances, it might not even be necessary. It all depends on your work style and professional requirements.

If your projects remain in the computer domain, where you're not relying on a mixer for anything other than monitoring your mix, you're probably smart to bounce the project directly to a format that you can burn from the internal CD-R burner. This process is the most efficient and in many cases sounds great.

As your recording proficiency and technical expectations increase, you'll want to experiment with printing your mixes to an analog recorder or through high-quality converters to a high-definition audio format. Keep pressing ahead to create better music, higher-quality audio, and more powerful mixes.

Digital Mix Recorders

One tool that I've found to be very useful in my work is a stand-alone CD recorder. This is a very easy and efficient way to record a reference copy to run out to the car for a real-life assessment of the mix or to send home with a client. When I go into mastering, I also take copies of all mixes from the CD recorder along with all other formats, just in case the CD sounds the best (it's never happened, yet, but it might) or in case something goes wrong with all the other formats and the CD is the only thing left to work with (this hasn't happened yet either, but somehow I still feel better knowing I have multiple redundancies).

When connecting any digital recorder to your digital system, you need to choose whether to use a digital or analog connection. Digital connections usually produce the best-sounding results, especially when there's no need for data format conversion. The choice you make should be based on assessment of all options. Some soundcard analog outputs simply don't sound good—they're virtually worthless. You won't know about your system until you listen critically to the results of differing connection scenarios. It's usually best to keep audio in the digital domain for all transfers, finally converting to analog only when necessary for monitoring, and using the highest-quality D/A converters available.

Analog Mix Recorders

If you're printing your mix via a digital connection to a CD recorder and the recorder is performing a real-time data conversion from a high-definition source (48/16 and above) to standard CD resolution

(44.1/16), be sure to listen to the results. Real-time data conversion often produces poor results. If your source is in high-definition audio format, you might realize better results by connecting the analog output from the console to the analog input of the CD recorder. Listen, assess, decide!

When I take a project into mastering, the format that almost always sounds best is analog two-track on 1/2-inch tape. Simply connect the analog outputs from your mixer or audio interface to the inputs of the analog recorder. Once you're in the analog domain, you'll need to pay closer attention to the mix levels. When you use an analog recorder, you'll probably be metering on standard VU meters. Audio signals are often easy to read on digital peak meters, yet difficult to read on VU meters. You might need to adjust mix levels for a more consistent reading on VU meters in the analog domain.

If you live in or near a large city, check into studio equipment rental. I don't really want to own an Ampex ATR-102 1/2-inch analog mix recorder; however, frequently I need to print mixes I do at home to that format. I have a couple places where I can rent excellent machines that are in great shape and well-maintained. The client pays for the rental, and I don't have to store or maintain the equipment. Once you've established a relationship with a rental facility, you'll be amazed at what you can rent on a daily, weekly, or monthly basis. Always weigh what you have with what you really need. Choose the best tools for the job and don't let the fact that you might not own them get in the way. Rental is a standard procedure, even in the large world-class studios. It's not efficient to own every piece of gear.

Networking Music Computers

Bus Connections

Data transfer rates are important factors in the efficiency of any digital audio, digital video, or other digital multimedia system. You can have the fastest computer on the planet, but if your device-to-device communication is performed through an inefficient transfer bus, you'll be in for some heartache. High-quality digital audio and video files are huge. As audio and video have become increasingly interwoven, and with the advent of massive playback media, such as DVD, bus speeds are more critical than ever. The following description of various transfer protocols provides a striking comparison.

SDS

Sample Dump Standard (SDS) is a protocol designed to facilitate transfer of digital audio samples and sustain loop information between sampling devices.

This data transfer process has been commonly adapted by individual manufacturers to their own systems. Therefore, communication between devices with different brand names isn't usually possible. However, a good computer-based sample editor software package can typically translate sample information for shared use between manufacturer-specific formats.

This protocol is snail-like when it comes to speed, clocking in at around 31,250 bits/second—the MIDI standard serial data transfer rate.

SCSI/Fast and Wide SCSI-2 and SCSI-3

The *small computer systems interface (SCSI)* offers a marked increase in data transfer speed over the SDS protocol. Each edition of the SCSI advancement has gotten faster and more capable. SCSI protocol includes some minimal processing on the actual interface board, making it a smarter system than the IDE/ATA protocol. It is also a more standardized system, so most SCSI-capable devices can cross-communicate. SCSI capacity and speed have increased dramatically over the last few years.

As the size and speed of these drives has increased (SCSI-3), they have been able to keep ahead of the capacity of computer bus speeds. The theoretically limit of the SCSI drive's data transfer rate is much faster than current drives. Therefore, when using new-technology SCSI drives, potential drive speed is not the limiting factor.

IDE/ATA

On an *IDE (Integrated Drive Electronics)* drive, the controller is integrated into the drive mechanism. The terms *IDE* and *ATA* are interchangeable. As with the SCSI-3 drives, drive speed isn't the limiting factor in most systems. As bus speeds increase, expect drive speeds to increase. It's most important to keep current with your computer and drive technology. Demands and expectations of computer speeds and capabilities increase frequently. In fact, since the '70s speeds and capacities have doubled about once every 18 months or so.

FireWire

The FireWire protocol, developed by Apple and applicable to both the Mac and PC formats, was adopted by the Institute of Electrical and Electronics Engineers (IEEE) as IEEE 1394, the industry-standard serial data bus. With transfer rates up to 800 megabits/second, the FireWire 800 protocol is a powerful tool in the arsenal of audio, video, and multimedia production.

The FireWire protocol offers several powerful and useful features:

+ It is a digital interface that doesn't require conversion to and from analog, therefore ensuring the most reliable signal integrity.

+ The standard defines 100-, 200-, 400-, and 800-mbps speeds, devices can support multiple speeds on a single bus.

+ FireWire supports freeform daisy-chaining and branching of up to 63 devices to your Mac or PC using small, thin serial-connecting cables of up to 14 feet in length.

+ Each device is hot-pluggable. They don't need to be turned off to connect and disconnect, and your computer doesn't need to be restarted when you make a device change.

+ The protocol auto-configures, with no need for device IDs, jumpers, dip switches, screws, latches, or terminators.

+ It supports guaranteed delivery of time-critical data, enabling smaller, low-cost buffers.

+ It supports two fundamental types of data transfer: asynchronous and isochronous. For traditional computer load and store applications, asynchronous, or nonsynchronized, transfers are adequate. Isochronous data transfer provides guaranteed data transport at a predetermined rate. This is especially important for multimedia applications where uninterrupted transport of time-critical data and just-in-time delivery reduce the need for costly buffering.

This type of speed revolutionizes the capabilities for multimedia production, integration with consumer electronics, and instantaneous access to multiple data sources.

Network and Online Data Transfer Rates

There's an amazingly high degree of integration of music and audio into networks and the Internet. Any recordist must not only be familiar with the options available, but must also strive to optimize these media as they apply to recording, data sharing, and communication. Using the correct tools in this area provides opportunity for timesaving file transfers and financially beneficial working arrangements. Comparison and evaluation of the functionality and pertinence of each protocol is fundamental to our effectiveness. Optimization of a setup in this regard provides a comfortable, stress-free, and productive working platform.

LocalTalk

LocalTalk is an outdated cabling scheme used to transmit AppleTalk information between Macintosh computers, printers, and other network devices. Its maximum transfer rate is 230,400 bits per second over a twisted-pair wire, not nearly enough to be useful in today's network applications.

AppleTalk

AppleTalk is the Mac network communication protocol accessed over an ethernet connection. Its speed capacity is dependent on the speed of the ethernet connection.

Ethernet

Ethernet is a protocol that connects computers and peripherals like printers, scanners, high-speed modems, and network devices. The speed of these connections has grown from 10 mbps, through 100 mbps, and on to 1 Gbps (referred to as *gigbit ethernet*). With these increases in speed, CPUs can be connected together to share processing power and data in real time, as though they were one computer. This is especially interesting when building an expandable system. If you've reached the processing power and speed capacity on one system, simply add another CPU and divide the workload accordingly between multiple CPUs. For demanding multimedia projects, this technology is dramatically beneficial.

Phone Modem

Typically the maximum phone modem data transfer rate is 56,000 bits/second, although the limiting factor is the quality of the phone line. Poor-quality phone lines can limit the transfer rate to less than 40,000 bits/second. Slow speeds like these make downloading and uploading on the Internet a grueling and painful task. In addition, the phone modem occupies a phone line and requires logging on and off for normal use.

If you transfer many files at all, you could literally save yourself hours in download and upload time by connecting via a high-speed cable or DSL. The motto: Lose the phone modem if at all possible!

High-Speed Cable and DSL Modems

High-speed cable Internet access is about 100 times faster than a 228,800-bits-per-second phone-line modem. This network uses the same cable television system that runs into most houses. At close to 3,000,000 bits per second, these systems are amazingly quick, include Internet access, and cost about the same as an extra telephone line and a typical Internet service provider.

ISDN (Integrated Services Digital Network)

Basically, ISDN provides a way to move more data over existing regular telephone lines. It can provide speeds of roughly 128,000 bits per second over regular telephone lines—in practice, most people will be limited to 56,000 or 64,000 bits per second. Cable modems and DSL connections have all but eliminated the need for ISDN connections in many areas, although there are still many areas around the world where this is a viable network option. Unlike dial-up, ISDN is a dedicated, always-on service and is available at speeds of 64 Kbps and 128 Kbps. Faster speeds of 256 Kbps and 512 Kbps can be obtained by bonding two and four ISDN lines, respectively.

T-1

T-1 is a leased-line connection capable of carrying data at 1,544,000 bits per second (1.544 Gbps). At maximum theoretical capacity, a T-1 line could move a megabyte in less than 10 seconds. However, that is still not fast enough for full-screen, full-motion video, for which you need at least 10,000,000 bits per second.

T-3

T-3 is a leased-line connection capable of carrying data at 44,736,000 bits per second (44.736 Gbps). This is more than fast enough to do full-screen, full-motion video. T-1 and T-3 connections are typically fiber-optic connections and contain several phone connections at slightly better than normal telephone bandwidth, along with very high-speed Internet access for multiple users.

Sharing Data

Networking computers has historically resulted in shared access to files and drives, network messaging, and some actual application and multimedia playback sharing. These functions are useful, though relatively simple and straightforward.

Apple Distributed Audio Processing

Apple has been an innovator in networking architecture for the home and studio audio recordist. Along with Apple Logic audio recording software, Apple has created distributed audio processing architecture, enabling single CPUs to work together through gigabit ethernet connections. All CPUs share the processing requirements in a way that not only feels like one computer, but also allows for virtually limitless expansion of the recording system. Steinberg offers a similar design in Nuendo.

A system like this lets a recording studio function in multiple rooms through a central network of CPUs. This technology even provides for the use of a laptop as the control over a large network of powerful computers, still keeping files on the laptop hard drive while utilizing the amazing power of the network, all connected via gigabit ethernet. Everything about this processing distribution is beneficial for recordists, from the home user who wants to seamlessly integrate with a commercial facility to the major commercial studio that needs the utmost in power and capacity.

Pro Tools Large Systems

Digidesign and the Pro Tools systems have addressed system expansion by creating several hardware devices that run in sync with the master computer and share the processing for specific functions. Though this type of system is not nearly as flexible as Apple's distributed processing network, it has provided a means to create a huge and complex high-definition recording system.

The advantage of the Pro Tools systems is that each processor is specifically designed for a purpose, including inputs, outputs, and other connections. These systems provide professional results and expandabilty. The disadvantage of the Pro Tools systems, especially for the home user or small studio, is cost. Each piece of a large system is expensive and the overall cost of a professional-level system is impressive.

Plug-Ins

This is a truly amazing horizon we stand at in the history of audio and multimedia production. Processors are so much faster than they've ever been, and disk storage space and options have become massive and plentiful. Music production is a cyclical event, where music serves technology and then technology serves music. It seems like we all need to get a bunch of new toys and play with them until we've used them up—and not until then do we really know what we want in our next toy revisions.

The music industry is giving us a lot of new tools, and many of them are in the second or third revision. Finally, in this cycle it's time for manufacturers to produce products based on musical needs again. It's a faultless system whereby products are manufactured with the mindset of, "This is new and cool, and let's see what's mathematically possible with this algorithm." Eventually we get around to, "We better get this to do what the musicians want it to do or we might go out of business."

Plug-ins are some of the newest audio toys for the masses, although they've been developing for a number of years. Two major factors have resulted in the increased popularity of audio recording plug-ins:

1. Processor speed – They require a lot of processor power and speed to function at a tolerable level. Only recently have CPUs become fast enough to run more than a few plug-ins at once in real time.

2. Additional hardware – Until the introduction of new very high-speed computers, any intensive use of plug-ins required additional hardware, such as the extensive line of plug-in support hardware from Digidesign for their Pro Tools systems. This stuff is great but it is pretty expensive for the average home or small studio user.

In Digidesign's defense, they've been servicing the upper echelon of commercial studios, who demand and can justify the best possible product. In the last few years Digidesign has addressed the home market with products such as the 002 and Mbox.

The Concept of Software Plug-Ins

The plug-in industry is growing incredibly. To explain all of the functions of each plug-in manufactured would not be productive, and the information would be relevant for only a limited amount of time. Instead, we are going to study the basic functionalities and capabilities of plug-ins. This information will remain classic and useful for some time to come.

A software plug-in operates and communicates within the framework of the host application—it plugs in to the existing package and increases its power and creative capacity. It augments the features of the software package through the implementation of additional effects, virtual instruments, and audio analysis tools.

Plug-ins provide a way for you to customize the capabilities of your system to specifically meet the needs of your recording and production style. The beauty of this concept is that a plug-in that one person uses regularly, fulfilling their every musical whim, might offer nothing to another user with a different creative style. Therefore, one user doesn't have to pay the extra price for the manufacturer building every possible tool into the basic software package, yet each user gets to invest in exactly the product that suits his or her musical need.

How to Handle Increased Demands on Your CPU and Drives

When you're producing audio on a computer there are a few basic rules that apply to every situation. These rules become even more important when you include real-time plug-ins. You must continually evaluate the status and effectiveness of:

+ Your computer processor and speed

+ The demands placed on your system by software, hardware, and plug-ins

+ The speed and compatibility of your storage devices compared to the needs of your audio production

+ The amount of RAM in your system and the real requirements for your production activities

Keep up with technology. Update your computer system when something newer and faster comes out. Minor revisions don't really count; nonetheless, when major chip changes occur, it's inevitable that your music software will soon be written to take advantage of increased speed and capacity. Wait for just one thing—wait until you know your software supports the technological change.

Keep up on free and paid upgrades to your software and plug-ins. Anything that's glitchy for you is probably glitchy for a lot of people. If you're having particular problem, write down everything about the problem that you can ascertain, then let tech support know what you've discovered. The newest upgrades almost always address reported functional issues and system incompatibilities.

Maintain your hard drives and other storage devices. Defragment on a regular basis and avoid operating with full drives. All hard drives work better when there is ample free disk space. Archive old files and keep the information on your drives pertinent to current projects—your system will love you for it.

RAM has gotten very inexpensive, although RAM price is cyclical—it definitely goes up and down. Keep your eye on the price of RAM. When it's down, that's the time to stock up. Your audio recording software will operate more efficiently as you increase available RAM.

Real-Time and Rendered Plug-Ins

There are two common plug-ins used in audio production: real-time and rendered. The actual way you implement these valuable tools isn't always a matter of personal choice or working style—it's often a matter of the processing capacity of your system.

Real-Time Plug-Ins

Real-time plug-ins are active during playback and recording. Essentially, they function just like an outboard hardware processor. They receive an input while the transport is in motion and they create the effect and output it in real time. Real-time plug-ins provide ultimate creative freedom because you can change parameters while the mix runs. You get to fine-tune the sound in context while you listen to your audio tracks.

The only problem with real-time plug-ins is that they increase the demand on your system by as much five times. The ability of your system to keep up with digital audio recording and playback while running real-time plug-ins is quickly tested. Sometimes it passes, sometimes it fails. Even as computer and drive speeds increase, we're usually on the edge, ready to max out almost anything the computer industry releases.

If you're seriously recording (especially high-definition audio), you'll need a multi-processor CPU with the newest, fastest chips. There isn't much of an option. The functionality of your system for audio recording is dependent the data transfer rate required for the sample and bit rates you choose, along with the number of tracks you want to include. Your CPU data bus and the drive you choose must be able to support the math of your needs.

It's pretty simple to calculate the basic transfer rate needed for any number of tracks at whatever resolution you desire. Simply consider the obvious factors: number of tracks (T), sample rate in kilobytes (R), and bit rate in kilobytes (B). For calculations, you must also consider that a kilobyte is actually 1024 bytes, so the result of the simple math must be divided by 1.024. So we derive the equation: $T \times R \times B \div 1.024$.

For a single track recorded at 44.1 kHz and 16-bit (2 bytes), the equation to determine the required transfer rate is $1 \times 44.1 \times 2 \div 1.024$. The result of this equation implies about 86-kB/second transfer rate is required per track at CD audio resolution. Considering that many CPU data buses transfer data in excess of 100 MBps and FireWire 800 has a potential transfer rate of nearly 100 MBps, a few tracks of CD-quality audio shouldn't be much of a problem for even an archaic computer (you know…anything more than a few years old).

Also, keep in mind that theoretical limits relating to computers and drives aren't always reality. There are other factors involved in the data stream. In actuality, a FireWire 800 drive that has a mathematical transfer rate of 100 MBps might only realize a functional transfer rate of 60 MBps. These factors change as technology changes, so read your specifications carefully.

Using this same equation, let's consider the basic transfer rate of a 24-track recording at a 24-bit, 192 kHz resolution. Simply plug in the variables. 24 (T) x 192 (R) x 3 (B) ÷ 1.024 = 13,500 kB, which equals a data rate requirement of 13.5 MBps. Start adding plug-ins to this kind of recording, and your requirements might approach 70 MBps.

The fact is, the amount of drain on your system is completely dependent on the plug-ins and recording software you use. In addition to your audio needs, your computer deals with its own OS along with software disc requirements, all open applications, system requirements, etc. Music software becomes more powerful with each revision, and therefore it places more demand on the CPU and drives. The same thing happens with plug-ins—they become more and more powerful and, at the same time, more and more demanding.

If you are maxing out your system with multiple plug-ins there is a solution—you must render some or all of the data.

Rendered Plug-Ins

Most current plug-ins will run in real time along with audio playback. In addition, plug-ins can be rendered or applied to the track. In this process, a region of audio is selected, then the plug-in effect is selected by previewing the affected audio. The preview process actually plays back the selected audio region through the plug-in so the effect is heard just as it will be applied. Once the effect is selected, the parameters are set, and the process is okayed, a new track is generated with the effect included. This track is then heard in place of the old track.

The upside of this process is that once the effect is rendered, the plug-in can be closed so it won't continue to tax the system. The downside of this process is that since you don't listen to the complete track while choosing effects, all parameter settings are guesses. You don't know until you play back the rendered audio track exactly how it fits in the mix. It might take several attempts to render the perfect rendition. Though this process can be cumbersome, it does provide a means to use lots of plug-ins on a system that is not capable of running them in real time.

Often, when I'm running several real-time plug-ins and I've got them just how I want them, I'll go ahead and render several tracks at once just to decrease the drain on the system. This works especially well on large groups of backing vocals, and it is very convenient to condense 20 or 30 tracks down to a well-blended stereo pair—the system gets a big break and you can divert your focus to more needy details.

Drives and RAM

Hard Drives

One rule: Get the fastest, biggest drive you can! You should keep your applications on one drive and record all of your audio files to a separate drive. There are so many instances when your software needs to access the drive for certain functions that it's best to avoid any possible conflict by specifying a drive just for audio.

Choose at least a 7,200-rpm drive—faster is even better. Fast SCSI, IDE, ATA, and FireWire drives all have the capacity to record loads of audio. Drive speed is competitive these days, so most manufacturers are producing suitable drives. For audio and other multimedia applications, choose a drive from a reputable manufacturer, either 7,200 or 10,000 rpm, with the Oxford 911 or 922 chip set.

RAM

One rule: Get lots of RAM! If you have plenty of RAM in your computer, the applications will store most necessary functional data in RAM. If there isn't enough RAM, the applications must access the hard drive for certain software and system tasks. The continual interaction between the applications and the hard drive can slow any process to a crawl. If you want your system to feel like a high-performance sports car, get lots of RAM.

Get good RAM. Some manufacturers highly recommend that you buy RAM from them, and they say that it's the best. Good RAM is RAM that works. If you're putting together a complex system and it's immediately going into an intense production environment, go ahead and get the manufacturer's RAM. They've tested it and will stand behind anything that might happen while you're using it.

I've had good experiences using manufacturer's specified RAM and I've had good experiences using the least expensive, yet correct, mail-order RAM. On two occasions I've gotten bad RAM—both were through mail order. In both cases, the companies immediately sent good RAM, but it was a hassle.

When I put together a new system I use the manufacturer-specified RAM. When I'm adding another gigabyte or so to increase an existing and functional system, I go the least expensive route because I'm not risking downtime.

Fragmentation

When data is written to the drive, it fills in gaps where other data used to be. It isn't automatically written in contiguous blocks with the priority that all data be easy to read quickly for the efficiency of our audio recording systems. It's written with the intent of getting the most information on the disc.

The result of this process is that your audio data might be scattered (fragmented) randomly all over the disk. In addition, applications and plug-ins could be written throughout the disk. When data is split up and written in multiple disk locations, its access time increases and response time decreases. When your system slows down and operates erratically, your disk is probably fragmented. The more fragmentation, the worse your system feels.

Occasionally you should use a program like Norton Disk Utilities to check the status of your disk and to perform a defragmentation routine. This process actually rewrites the disk data so that applications and files are grouped together in the most efficient manner. All application and system data are grouped together and all files are written into contiguous sections, leaving leftover disk space available in one large section. This is a great way to achieve the quickest and most efficient access to data. Once the disk has been defragmented, you'll be amazed at how much better your system runs.

The Benefits of Software Plug-Ins

Software plug-ins consolidate your musical and textural palette. Without having to patch in any other device, you get the benefit of an increased textural arsenal. Plug-ins used along with a very powerful and fast computer can simulate the inclusion of an impressive additional rack of effects with several powerful sound modules.

Real-time software plug-ins usually accommodate automation control from the built-in automation in your recording software. This is a creative bonus to the already impressive combination of software and plug-ins.

As with any software-based system, upgrades help keep your tools effective and functional over the years. New versions are released and, as if by magic, you have a new set of functions, and the original functions are probably better than they ever were. Some upgrades are free; some come at a minimal upgrade charge. This is a great way to keep your system as current as possible. I've probably been using Auto-Tune by Antares longer than any other third-party plug-in. It keeps getting better and it has kept up with my OS changes, processor changes, and musical needs.

Plug-In Formats

Plug-in formats are still in the process of standardizing. Several different manufacturers have developed their own rendition of plug-in formats and some of them have become very popular; however, it will take us a while to see complete integration and agreement on plug-in protocol.

Once you install a plug-in in your system, it will function with any application that recognizes your plug-in format. This is a very convenient feature, allowing the user to get the most out of his or her software purchase. For example, I use the T.C. Electronic PowerCore on my PowerBook under the Apple Units format. The complete package of T.C. plug-ins is available on all music programs I use on the PowerBook, whether Digital Performer, Pro Tools, Nuendo, or GarageBand.

Windows Plug-In Formats

The following list of plug-in formats shows the currently compatible audio recording software for each plug-in format for both Windows and Mac.

TDM

TDM plug-ins work with Pro Tools and Pro Tools LE.

TDM *(Time Division Multiplexing)* is a Digidesign Pro Tools development designed to facilitate the expansion of their recording systems and the incorporation of their Pro Tools hardware options. Other manufacturers are beginning to recognize the TDM format. In fact, some manufacturers, such as Apple Logic and MOTU, are structuring their software so that it will function seamlessly as the front-end user interface for large and small Pro Tools systems.

RTAS

RTAS works with Pro Tools and Pro Tools LE.

RTAS is another Digidesign format, used typically with the smaller systems that don't include extra hardware. RTAS stands for *Real Time AudioSuite.*

AudioSuite

AudioSuite plug-ins work with Pro Tools and Pro Tools LE.

AudioSuite plug-ins have been part of the most basic core Pro Tools system for years. Though limited in the scope, their useful tools give the user a taste of the convenience and power of plug-ins.

HTDM

HTDM plug-ins work with Pro Tools TDM-based systems.

HTDM stands for *host-TDM,* which means they derives all of their processing power from the host computer. There is no use of external hardware DSP to operate the plug-ins.

DirectX

DirectX plug-ins work with Sound Forge, Acid, Vegas, CD Architect, WaveLab, Audition, Cakewalk, SONAR Producer Edition, Cubase SX, and Nuendo.

DirectX protocol was developed by Microsoft and enjoys a large base of primarily PC/Windows users.

VST

VST plug-ins work with Cubase SX, Nuendo, WaveLab (Audio Montage). This is probably the most widely used format to date.

Apple OS X Plug-In Formats

TDM

TDM plug-ins for Mac work with Pro Tools and Pro Tools LE, Apple Logic Audio, and Digital Performer.

RTAS

RTAS plug-ins work with Pro Tools and Pro Tools LE. This format is typically used with the smaller systems that don't include extra hardware.

AudioSuite

Audio Suite plug-ins work with Pro Tools, Pro Tools LE, Logic Audio, and Digital Performer.

HTDM

HTDM plug-ins work with Pro Tools.

Audio Units

Audio Units plug-ins work with Logic Audio, GarageBand, Peak, SPARK XL, and Digital Performer.

VST

VST plug-ins work with Cubase SX, Nuendo, Peak, and SPARK XL.

MAS

MAS (*MOTU Audio System*) plug-ins work exclusively with Mark of the Unicorn products (primarily Digital Performer).

The Pioneers of Plug-Ins

Plug-ins started out around 1995 as a result of Web browser developers implementing a system to provide multimedia support, adding functionality outside the host application. Music, layout, science, art, and graphics software developers almost immediately adopted this concept. In today's software market and into the future, plug-ins are an important part of the power available in production. Artists, developers, scientists…virtually everyone can customize the software they use to fit the way they work.

Most of the plug-in formats offer very similar features and capabilities. In fact, virtually all plug-in manufacturers support the majority of available application formats. However, TDM was the first workstation-based technology to offer:

+ Access to a complete suite of processors across multiple channels

+ Non-destructive, real-time effects available during recording or playback

- Automation of plug-in parameters

Digidesign offers some plug-ins, but the majority of TDM plug-ins are produced and distributed by other manufacturers. This third-party boon has been fueled over the years by an amazing demand from Pro Tools users.

The Two Operational Types of Plug-Ins

Native Processing-Based Plug-Ins

Native processing-based plug-ins use the existing processing power of the host CPU. They save the expense of adding additional DSP hardware and have become very popular with the advent of each newer and faster generation of computer.

The downside with native plug-ins is the lack of expandability. Once the CPU is maxed out, that's the end of the road until you get a faster computer or add hardware. The upside is that you can get a lot of creative power out of a current computer and native plug-ins.

DSP Hardware-Based Plug-Ins

Compared to native processing, DSP hardware-based systems are more costly. Your need for video cards or accelerators might get in the way of your desire to add hardware, since most hardware additions occupy one of the PCI or other expansion slots in the CPU. A maxed-out Pro Tools system could easily also use up all of your computer's PCI expansion slots.

PCI Hardware

The upside to DSP-based systems is truly in system expandability without increased demand on the CPU. This leaves the computer processors free to perform at their optimum, running software and plug-in interfaces with the additional hardware.

The only real downside is cost. It's difficult to justify the cost of additional hardware unless your system is in frequent, gainful use.

Because of the hardware connection to the PCI slot, any integration with a laptop requires an expansion system that provides access to PCI slots. Magma Mobile Electronics, Inc. offers a CardBus-to-PCI system that works on Mac or PC.

FireWire Hardware

There are several excellent products available that connect via FireWire. A system like this is perfect for laptop- or desktop-based systems. If you are using a tower or desktop system, PCI-based hardware will provide better expandability and overall power. Considering that you'll probably want to include external FireWire drives, it's typically better to share the bus load by using both the PCI expansion lots and the FireWire bus, rather than running everything through the FireWire bus.

Several manufacturers have addressed the convenience and popularity of FireWire interfaces. Digidesign, MOTU, T.C. Electronic, and others produce excellent products.

Listen to the following Audio Examples of the T.C. Electronic PowerCore FireWire interface. It is connected to my PowerBook with a multitracked drum set recorded dry. All effects are from the PowerCore and are performed without additional drain on the laptop processor.

Audio Example 7-1

FireWire Plug-In Hardware

Video Example 7-1

PowerCore FireWire Hardware-Based System

Latency

Latency has traditionally been an issue with plug-in use. It is the time delay induced by software processing. If your system is slow or a little older you might notice a slight delay in audio that is being processed by a plug-in. This latency occurs to a greater degree when real-time processing is being used.

Most manufacturers have developed data processing schemes that claim zero latency—no time delay between onset and delivery of the audio data. This requires a very fast computer and the most up-to-date software and hardware.

Latency is an issue in any data stream. MIDI protocol has a built-in latency of about three milliseconds. The amount of audio latency in a system is completely dependent on the software, drives, hardware, processor, and bus speed, as well as the complexity of the data being manipulated.

The Five Functional Types of Plug-Ins

There are five basic functional types of plug-ins: track-based, bus-based, mix-based, analysis, and virtual instrument. Even though one type of plug-in might be most commonly used for a specific functional application, that doesn't mean it can't be creatively used for any of the other functional applications.

Track-Based Plug-Ins

Track-based plug-ins insert into the digital signal path of one single track. Functionally, these software plug-ins are like the dynamics processors in the analog domain that typically effect one track. Software plug-ins that should be used on individual tracks are typically all the dynamics plug-ins, such as compressors, limiters, gates, expanders, de-essers, and exciters. In addition, it's common to apply equalization and tuning plug-ins to individual tracks.

Video Example 7-2

Using Track-Based Plug-Ins

Bus-Based Plug-Ins

A bus-based plug-in is used whenever you need to use the same effect on multiple tracks. Reverberation effects are most often used in conjunction with an aux bus. With this system, set up your virtual mixer with aux sends on each channel of the virtual mixer, then turn up the send on whatever track needs the effect. Next route the aux bus to the plug-in input and the output of the plug-in to the mixer input. Often, effects plug-ins default their outputs directly into the stereo mix, so patching back into the mixer is unnecessary.

Most software recording packages provide ample aux buses just for this type of use.

Video Example 7-3

Using Bus-Based Plug-Ins

Mix-Based Plug-Ins

Mix-based plug-ins are inserted after the main stereo or surround mix output—they affect the entire mix. The most common example of this type of plug-in is the mastering plug-in. Mastering plug-ins are designed to limit and/or equalize the entire mix, specifically to increase mix loudness and power. Specialized mastering limiters and equalizers like those provided by Waves, Universal Audio, and T.C. Electronic produce excellent results that dramatically increase the impact of your music. Most audio recording software packages include limiters and equalizers that serve these functions well, but third-party plug-ins specialize in one specific task and typically perform it with a more polished and professional edge than stock plug-ins.

Video Example 7-4

Using Mix-Based Plug-Ins

Analysis Plug-Ins

Analysis plug-ins are also often inserted at the end of the mix chain, but their function is to provide quantification of the mix content. They typically display EQ content, and in the case of real-time analyzer (RTA) plug-ins they might indicate perceived loudness compared to actual signal level, or they might display phase information between the mix channels. Analysis plug-ins are often used in conjunction with mastering plug-ins. Usually, mastering plug-ins are the tools used to fix the problems indicated by analysis plug-ins.

Video Example 7-5

Using Analysis Plug-Ins

Virtual Instrument Plug-Ins

Virtual instrument plug-ins are essentially like adding a synthesizer, drum machine, or sound module to your system without needing to actually add a keyboard or other hardware. These useful plug-ins add dramatically to the power and creative scope of your basic software package. Instruments play back on your regular mixer channels and offer virtually every instrument and sound you could imagine.

The processing power available in your CPU typically dwarfs the available power that resides in a keyboard or sound module, so the sounds produced by virtual instruments can be amazing. Sound quality and musical relevance is in the ear of the beholder and at the mercy of the software developer.

Video Example 7-6

Using Virtual Instrument Plug-Ins

Wrappers

Wrappers are simply translators between plug-in formats. If your recording software doesn't support VST plug-ins, yet you want to use some of the countless VST plug-ins available in both free and not-free forms, search for a VST wrapper on Google and you'll get a long list of options. You can usually find a wrapper fairly quickly that works with your recording software and translates to most other plug-in formats.

Wrappers have gotten fairly stable, although they're not always dependable with all plug-ins. Even though they might be a little glitchy with some plug-ins, they still provide access to more creative tools.

Finding and Choosing Plug-Ins

One thing is incredibly amazing about the plug-in market. On one hand, you can purchase incredible packages of world-class plug-ins, such as those produced by Waves, T.C. Electronic, Universal Audio, Spectrasonics, and many others for a fair although substantial amount of money. On the other hand, you can find countless freeware and shareware plug-ins available on the Internet for free!

Most freeware and shareware plug-ins are written in VST or DirectX format. It's also increasingly frequent to see Audio Units format. If you find a plug-in that doesn't match your format, download a wrapper to translate between formats.

These plug-ins are typically written by a wide range of programmers. If you run across a freeware or shareware plug-in that's exceptional, it might even be a test run by an excellent programmer, working up a new approach to musical production, or it could be the experiment of a talented programmer. You're also likely to find these plug-ins created by novices; they might be unstable, contain viruses, or adversely affect your complete system.

Freeware Plug-Ins

There are some very good free plug-ins available, especially when you consider the creative process. It could be that you're looking for a sonic impact that's different from the norm. In this case, even if the free plug-in didn't do what it was supposed to do, or didn't do it well, it might be just the right touch for your music.

A freeware application might be an excellent creative tool, it might sound good, it might sound bad, and it might never cause a problem. It also might make your system crash every time you use it, or it might just cause a gremlin to inhabit the machine, lurking quietly in the background, rearing its ugly head at the worst time, then slithering back into its hole to await the next grand moment.

Shareware Plug-Ins

Shareware is just the next notch above freeware. Sometimes these plug-ins are higher quality, sometimes not. The concept of shareware places a suggested price on the product. You can download and use it for free; however, if you actually end up liking and using the product, you should pay the programmer the suggested fee. This is a much-abused honor system. As with any creative activity, whether music, books, art, or software, if you're using the goods, you should pay for the goods.

Shareware carries most of the same dangers as freeware, but it's common to find a nice piece of shareware, or freeware for that matter, that doesn't have huge mass-market appeal but really fits the way you create. Just because there is a nominal fee for shareware, that doesn't necessarily mean it's a better product than freeware.

Blogs, Bulletin Boards, and User Groups

If you're going to get into shareware and freeware, search out a user group full of people who like to do what you like to do—they're all over. Google almost any topic and you'll find a blog, bulletin board, or user group that can't wait to tell you what they know about it. You can ask questions, answer questions, and generally take advantage of the collective group knowledge.

Joining one of these groups is a great way to find out which freeware or shareware is good or bad.

Making the Transition to Commercial Plug-Ins

Freeware and shareware plug-ins provide an excellent point of entry for the casual recordist. A lot can be learned about how plug-ins work and what the new user really wants. Nonetheless, when you want to get serious about the quality of audio and music you produce, step up to the plate and invest in some high-quality professional plug-ins. You won't be sorry. When you buy a plug-in that has been written by a top-level programmer for a company that knows exactly what they want in a product, you bypass a world of strife and pain. You get an industry-tested tool that's stable and sounds good.

Most top-level manufacturers spend great amounts of time and money testing and rewriting and working as a strong team to develop a superior product. It stands to reason that their product is vastly superior to the product of a part-time hobbyist programmer writing code while watching *American Idol*.

Daily, I use plug-ins by Waves, Antares, Universal Audio, T.C. Electronic, Spectrasonics, and other commercial manufacturers along with resident plug-ins that come with the host software. They are excellent! In fact, I'm amazed on a fairly regular basis at the capabilities of these plug-ins. Once in a while I'll download some freeware or shareware that catches my attention, but I almost never end up using it because it's unstable or I just don't end up liking how it sounds.

In addition to their sonic superiority and stability, don't overlook the support provided by a legitimate software plug-in manufacturer. If you're trying to produce the best possible audio, you will on occasion find a need for tech support—it can save the day and it can help you record better audio. Even though typically you can e-mail the developer when you find a bug, tech support is not really offered by freeware and shareware developers.

Internet Paid Download

Commercial plug-ins can often be purchased online in the form of a download. Documentation is provided electronically in PDF form, and registration is performed via one of a few different e-mail authorization schemes. I like buying software online because of the "I gotta have this right now" factor. If you purchase and receive documentation online it can be a challenge keeping track of everything. You'll need to develop some kind of filing system that organizes all of your online documentation and registration codes. Over the course of time, it's easy to lose random files on your desktop.

Hard Copy Packaged Plug-Ins

There's something really fun about getting all the hard copy documentation along with real install discs and authorization codes and all the pretty packaging. In this era of buying data, it feels like you're actually getting something for your money.

If you prefer to buy packaged software, keep careful track of your registration and authorization codes. They're typically in the front or back of the manual, but sometimes those are hard to find after a long period of time. If your hard drive goes bad or if you change computers, it takes enough time and energy to get all of your favorite applications back up and running without scrounging through piles of manuals in search of authorization codes. To make it really easy to reload most software, use a Sharpie to carefully write the code on all install disc. That way the code is right where you need it, when you need it. It's also a good idea to keep all of your install discs in a CD folder. They might go through various stages of organization or disorganization, but at least you'll always know where your install discs are, and the codes will be right there with them.

Mail Order or Music Store?

It is so often tempting to buy through mail order. You typically save on tax, and you get a great price because you're not paying for the overhead of a storefront. However, there is often no support offered. If something goes wrong, you're sent directly to the manufacturer, who will help you in due time. In their defense, some mail order companies offer support and perform an excellent service. Sweetwater is an example of a good online audio store. They specialize in audio products, and you're paired up with a salesperson who acts as your personal sales support for your purchases. They also have decent tech support.

I am a big fan of developing a relationship with a local music store. If you live in a metropolitan area, there's probably a good music store in your area with a knowledgeable salesperson. Find the head of the department, be friendly, and buy gear. You'll find one of your strongest allies in your recording life. I have one guy that I buy from first. If he doesn't have what I need, I'll call some other salespeople I know at other stores. He's very knowledgeable; he knows what I have, he knows what I'm looking for, and often he knows what I *should be* looking for rather than what I *am* looking for.

In Seattle, we have a number of excellent audio dealers. They're really all great and perform a great service. They realize that they're competing against mail order and that the product they offer that mail order can't compete with is personal service. It's the same all over the world. You need a person you can call who can help you with your product. If you're new to plug-ins, you need someone to help you through the maze. If they can't help you, they can streamline the path to help.

Another benefit of working with a local salesperson is that salespeople attend national conferences such as NAMM (*National Association of Music Merchandisers*) and they see new and improved products a couple times a years, plus they get constant calls from their suppliers to keep them up to date on everything that's new. You might actually end up buying something that's outdated or obsolete without that human support you get from a real person.

The Plug-Ins

Almost all plug-ins are available in all formats, so whether you choose DSP-based or native-based plug-ins, you have many creative tools readily available. The following section demonstrates the sound and functions of several plug-ins. These are plug-ins I use on regular basis. I don't want this to seem like an advertisement for these companies in particular. There are so many great plug-ins available that no one could ever show them all off. If you're new to plug-ins or just looking for other options, these examples should give you some help determining what might work for your creative style.

Listen to the following Audio Examples and watch the Video Examples to see and hear how these valuable tools function and sound.

Dynamics Plug-Ins

Waves

Waves offers some excellent dynamics plug-ins. Their Renaissance channel is very warm-sounding and smooth. Software plug-ins provide the option of weighting the frequency range of compression and other setups that are cumbersome to accomplish in the analog domain, yet simple in these plug-ins.

The Waves C1 provides a simple-to-use interface that is very graphical and user-friendly.

Universal Audio

Universal Audio has manufactured some of the most well-respected analog hardware for long enough to have vintage status placed on many of their pieces of gear. Rather than fade away, they embraced the digital era, creating software versions of their most popular hardware. They have done an amazing job of recreating the sonic effect of their classic

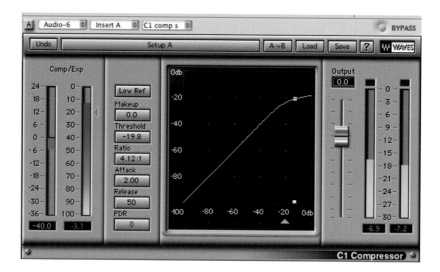

gear, and on top of all that, they've succeeded in creating a user interface that looks and feels like the original.

The UA 1176, Teletronix LA2A, and Pultec EPQ-1A are nothing short of spectacular. They also offer some excellent reverberation plug-ins, including the classic Plate 140.

These are great-sounding plug-ins and they look really cool! I've used UA hardware extensively for a long time and I love their plug-ins.

The Universal Audio plug-ins are hardware-based, using a UAD-1 PCI DSP card along with their software plug-ins. This combination increases the available power to the plug-ins while leaving the CPU more free to do the tasks it really needs to do.

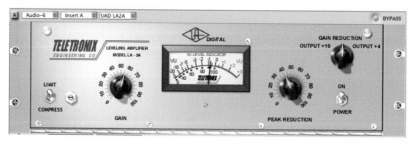

T.C. Electronic

The T.C. plug-ins are hardware-based, running from the PowerCore FireWire interface. T.C. has done a great job of building some very usable and wonderful-sounding plug-ins. The 247C compressor sounds good and looks good. It has the feel of a Universal Audio 1176 combined with the Teletronix LA2A. Another very powerful compressor from T.C. is the multi-band Dynamic EQ.

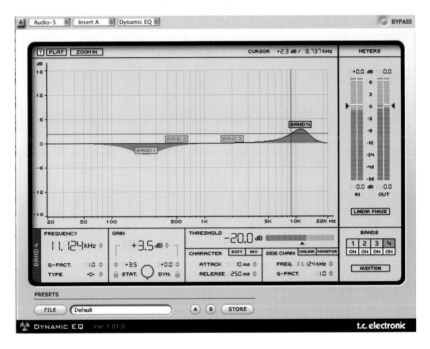

Video Example 7-7

Using the Waves C1, UA LA2A, and T.C. Dynamic EQ

Equalization Plug-Ins

Waves

The Waves Linear Phase EQ is a very clean and powerful six-band parametric equalizer.

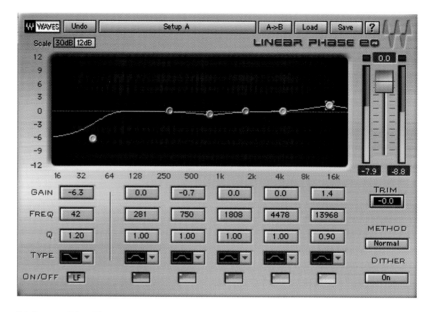

Universal Audio

The UA Precision Mastering Equalizer provides a vintage look and feel with a stereo four-band sweepable equalizer. A selectable high-pass filter cleans out the low end.

T.C. Electronic

The T.C. Electronic EQSAT Custom is a very powerful and flexible equalizer with great-sounding presets already programmed. The T.C. plug-ins are capable of producing high-definition, 96-kHz effects with no additional burden on the host CPU.

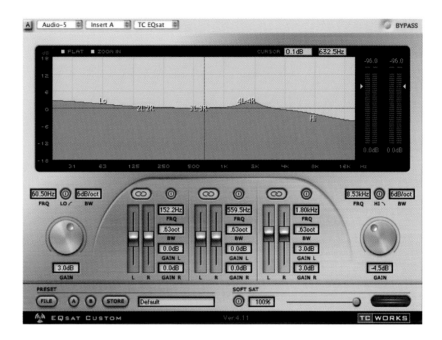

Video Example 7-8

Using the Waves Linear Phase EQ, UA Precision Mastering Equalizer, and T.C. EQSAT

Reverberation Effects

Waves IR-1 Convolution Reverb

Convolution reverberation plug-ins are very powerful and place a healthy demand on the CPU. This Waves convolution reverb sounds excellent and is capable of mimicking the sound of almost any natural acoustic space. However, you can't run too many of these plug-ins before your processor bogs down.

T.C. Electronic

T.C. Electronic is well known for its excellent reverberation algorithms. Their powerful MegaVerb 96k provides user-selectable parameters for room shape and size, as well as wall diffusion characteristics, and it sounds great, too.

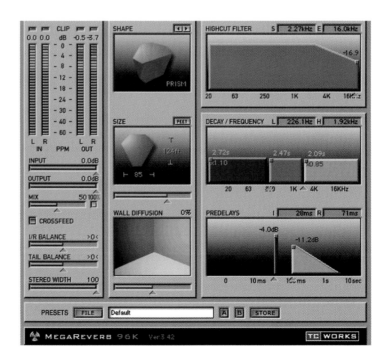

Using the Waves IR-1 Convolution Reverb and the T.C. MegaVerb 96K

Sound Effects Plug-Ins

Waves

With a digital signal path it's easy to route, combine, and modulate sounds in a way that isn't natural or even possible with regular hardware effects. The fact that these effect parameters are part of the automation data makes it possible for wild sweeps and effect changes to occur in rhythmic time and in sync with the music they support. The Waves Enigma is just one example of a powerful sound-shaping tool.

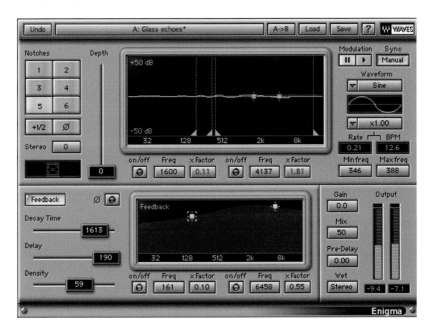

MOTU

MOTU actually includes a good set of plug-ins with Digital Performer. There is a good selection of dynamics and effects plug-ins, including Multimode Filter, which looks kind of like an old MultiMoog synth.

Video Example 7-10

Using the Waves Enigma and MOTU Multimode Filter

Tuning Plug-Ins

Tuning plug-ins are very powerful. They are effective on single-note sources, whether a vocal, lead guitar, violin, cello, bass, flute, or any other instrument that plays one note at a time.

Antares Auto-Tune

Auto-Tune is really an exceptional program. Since its arrival on the plug-in scene in the early days of plug-ins, Auto-Tune has been used, over-used, abused, and used again. The fact is, it does an awesome job of getting tracks in tune. Cher was one of the first artists to use this plug-in; she always had an intonation issue, but not with Auto-Tune. You choose the key for diatonic melodies or you can choose from chromatic, Ling Lung, 53-Tone, or any of the 29 user-selectable scales.

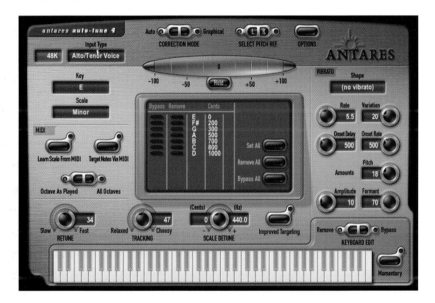

I use Auto-Tune a lot, but I prefer to set the parameters so that it gently rides the pitch. If there's a long note that drifts out of tune, I want Auto-Tune to save the day—and it does. Early on, it became popular to use Auto-Tune to make vocal pitch change with keyboard accuracy, each pitch jumping instantly to the next and locking perfectly in tune. I prefer the natural approach—at least today.

Virtual Instruments

Virtual instruments are an amazing addition to the recordist's tool kit. They typically contain great sounds and are played from a keyboard or any other MIDI input device that's connected to your system. There is an amazing amount of virtual instrument plug-ins available. You can find virtually all classic synths, wild creative tools that are like Swiss Army knives of instrument sounds, and simple little plug-ins that do one little thing. They're all just part of your creative palette to use and abuse as you please.

Spectrasonics

I love this company. Their sounds are awesome and they have some very musical and forward-thinking technological features. They offer three great plug-ins: Stylus RMX (drum grooves), Atmosphere (pads and synths), and Trilogy (bass module).

Stylus RMX

Stylus RMX provides tons of great drum and percussion sounds, with a really great array of expansion modules that are all very useful. They have developed a randomizing parameter, called Chaos, which changes the groove in the same way a live drummer might. By randomly throwing in the Chaos personality you control how wild the changes are—you can create a very real-sounding groove track. Stylus RMX also includes racks of effects, a mixer, and multiple creative functionalities—and it looks really cool.

Atmosphere Dream Synth

Atmosphere Dream Synth is like the ultimate pad synth. The sounds are great and the controls are powerful.

Trilogy Bass Module

The Trilogy Bass Module fills out the rhythm section. Along with Stylus RMX, this virtual instrument provides an awesome production tool.

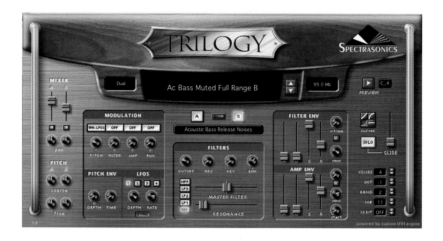

Video Example 7-12

Using Spectrasonics' Stylus RMX with Expansion Libraries

Guitar Plug-Ins

These plug-ins have become a category of their own. The sounds guitarists get out of vintage amps and effects are modeled and included in most of these plug-ins. Distortion sounds are very important to most guitar sounds. Most of the guitar plug-ins have great distortion and effect sounds, complete with miking technique choices. There are great plug-ins available from Line 6, Native Instruments, T.C. Electronic, and many others. The fact that these are made for guitarists doesn't mean they can't be used on other instruments or even voices.

Tubifex

T.C. Electronic Tubifex offers three tube simulation stages and detailed sound-shaping controls. A very powerful feature of guitar plug-ins is that you have the ability to record the direct guitar, leaving the final guitar sound choices for mixdown.

Video Example 7-13

Using the T.C. Tubifex

Mastering Plug-Ins

Mastering plug-ins let you polish your mixes after they're all done. Limiting is a primary mastering function. It's the limiting process that helps make your mix sound loud. Many mastering plug-ins contain peak limiting and equalization functions. When you're mastering an album, the EQ functions help shape the basic EQ characteristic of each song so that all the songs blend together into an album.

Waves L1, L2, and L3

The Waves L1, L2, and L3 Ultramaximizer limiters are very highly respected in the mastering industry. They sound great and they are very easy to use. The L3 Multimaximizer includes multiband compression, which helps shape the tonal characteristic while dynamically controlling each frequency range.

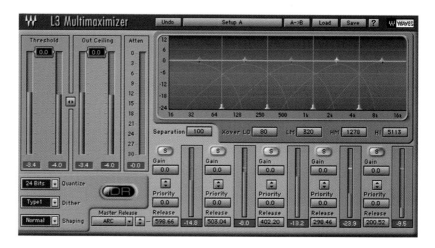

Universal Audio

For a more vintage approach to mastering, select some of the classic tools from the Universal Audio plug-ins. You might want to try the UA Precision Limiter into the Pultec EQP-1A Program Equalizer.

T.C. Electronic

The T.C. Master X3 is a powerful and precise multiband limiter. T.C. has done an excellent job of providing tools with precise control that sound and look good. I can't explain why it's so much more fun to use plug-ins that look good, too.

Video Example 7-14

Using the Waves L3 Multimaximizer, T.C. Master X3, and Universal Audio Precision Limiter into the Pultec EQP-1A Program Equalizer

Synchronization

Synchronization has become an increasingly complex process as technology has evolved. Modern-day equipment has so much flexibility and so many sync capabilities that constant study and updating is required of any serious recordist. We're in a constant state of anxiously awaiting the next amazing tool. Keeping current with technology is no longer good enough; we must continually be prepared for what's coming.

The basic concept of synchronizing hasn't changed since its inception. Musicians have always appreciated sharing the same groove—I'm sure of it. Synchronized swimmers know what each member of the team intends to do, and they keep track of each other without any of the audience realizing it so they can remain synchronized throughout the entire program.

Synchronizing recording equipment is similar to synchronizing musicians and swimmers:

- ◆ It's ideal if all gear is in exactly the same groove. It's easier to get everyone working together if all participants speak the same language.

- ◆ Some players, swimmers, and recording equipment are better at synchronizing accurately than others.

- ◆ Every once in a while, even the best have a bad day and, for unexplained reasons, mess up everybody that they're around.

In this chapter, we'll cover several different types of synchronization and how they might or might not work well together. Our goal is to understand all the ingredients in order to make informed and insightful decisions regarding system configurations and equipment purchase options.

Synchronizing Basics

Any synchronization system needs a master transport, which all others follow. Devices that follow the master are called *slaves*, and they must follow the master within the tightest sync tolerance possible. Different types of synchronization schemes offer varying degrees of accuracy. Some systems are relatively loose, with machines fading back and forth in relation to the master speed. Other, newer systems are able to remain locked to sample-accurate perfection. In a sample-accurate synchronization system, the machines are locked so tightly together that they act like one. If the master machine plays back at a sample rate of 48 kHz, so does the slave. The slave verifies at each sample that it's still in sync, and it doesn't drift at all.

In its infancy, the synchronization process was primal compared to our current capabilities. Early schemes, like *pilot tone*, were an attempt to control film transports so that audio and film images could be combined after the final film print was completed. As the film and television industries grew, SMPTE became an industry standard for synchronizing image to picture; it provided much more flexibility. The simple ability to start, stop, and resume playback at any point in a program while maintaining sync between all SMPTE-savvy machines was a boon. With modern synchronization methods and protocol, not only can many machines sync quickly and easily, but they can sync in a sample-accurate manner. Modern systems can synchronize many devices, representing hundreds of audio tracks, so that they act and sound like a single machine.

Time Code and Sync Pulse

What is time code? What is sync pulse? What does time code do and how does it work? First off, understand that sync pulse and time code are used to synchronize multiple machine-driven mechanisms, or timing clocks, so that all synchronized systems run at the same speed and in a constant relation to one another. Both sync pulse and time code are series of electronic pulses that are produced by a sequencer, drum machine, or time code generator. These pulses are typically recorded onto one track of an audio or video tape recorder. Later, the signal from the tape track is plugged into the sync in jack of the sequencer or machine synchronizer to serve as a tempo guide for future tracks. Sync pulse is the simplest and least flexible of these systems, but it is still common in lower-priced and older drum machines and sequencers. These principles pertain to synchronization of audio machines, video machines, film machines, sequencers, drum machines, and computers.

Synchronizing two sequencers means making their tempos match perfectly. Sync pulse can accomplish this. Time code can accomplish this with more control and flexibility.

Synchronizing two tape recorders means making their motors run at the same speed. A relative of sync pulse, called *pilot tone*, can accomplish this. Time code can accomplish this with more control and flexibility.

Synchronizing a sequencer to a tape recorder means enabling a sequencer to imitate and duplicate a tempo map in relation to parts recorded on tape. Sync pulse can accomplish this. Time code can accomplish this with more control and flexibility.

Sync Pulse

Sync pulse is the simplest synchronizing system. This system uses a specified number of electronic pulses per quarter note to drive the tempo of a sequencer. Most sync pulse is generated at 24 pulses per quarter note, and each pulse is identical. The only factor that establishes synchronization is how fast the pulses are being sent or received.

It's very simple. When a drum machine or sequencer is set to an external clock and a sync pulse is sent into the sync in jack, the tempo of the sequencer follows according to the rate of the sync pulse. Every time 24 pulses go by, the sequencer plays another quarter note's worth of your sequence. The faster the sync pulses, the faster the tempo. When you listen to the sound of sync pulse, you'll notice that the pitch of the sync tone raises and lowers as the tempo speeds up and slows down.

Sync pulse has one major disadvantage: Each pulse is identical. There is no way for this system to indicate to the sequencer which measure of the sequence should be playing. The sequencer always needs to hear the sync pulse from the beginning of the song to be precisely in sync with a previously recorded track.

Almost all sequencers that accept external clock information respond to sync pulse. Most newer equipment will also accept time code.

SMPTE/Time Code

Time code gives much more control and flexibility than sync pulse. The most common form of time code is SMPTE, pronounced *SIMP-tee*. The initials S-M-P-T-E stand for the Society of Motion Picture and Television Engineers. This society of professionals developed SMPTE time code as a means of interlocking (synchronizing) audio, video, and film transports.

A piece of equipment that produces SMPTE time code is said to generate time code. A piece of equipment that accepts and operates from time code is said to read time code. The time code reader and generator are almost always in the same piece of equipment, often with other MIDI functions and features.

Now that we have the formal introduction out of the way, this is how SMPTE works: This code is a continuous flow of binary information—a stream of constantly changing zeroes and ones that lasts for 24 hours before starting over. Each single point in time has its own unique binary number. These unique binary numbers are referenced to a 24-hour clock. This gives us a way of pinpointing a particular position in the flow of the code. Each point in the code has a unique address that's described in hours, minutes, seconds, frames, and sometimes sub-frames. The term *frame* comes from the film world, which calls each picture in the film a frame.

SMPTE time code is generated at a constant speed. Tempo isn't changed by the time code speeding up and slowing down; tempo is changed by the sequencer calculating where the song should be in relation to the time code's 24-hour clock. The 24-hour SMPTE clock

SMPTE Time Code

A particular point in the flow of SMPTE time code might be indicated by a number like 01:32:51:12. This number indicates the song position at 1 hour, 32 minutes, 51 seconds, and 12 frames.

If a device is set to start a song at SMPTE reference 01:32:51:12, then as the sequencer receives the continuous flow of time code, it waits until that exact set of code numbers comes up to play beat 1 of measure 1 of the song.

Time code is a 24-hour clock. It runs from 00:00:00:00 to 23:59:59:29 before it starts over again at 00:00:00:00.

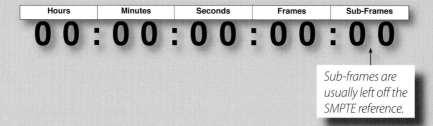

Hours	Minutes	Seconds	Frames	Sub-Frames

$$0\,0 : 0\,0 : 0\,0 : 0\,0 : 0\,0$$

Sub-frames are usually left off the SMPTE reference.

runs from 00:00:00:00 to 23:59:59:29 before it starts over again at 00:00:00:00.

If a sequence is set to external sync and is set to start at 1 hour, 20 minutes, and 10 seconds (01:20:10:00), beat 1 of measure 1 of the sequence will play at 01:20:10:00. All tempo settings and changes are controlled within the sequencer, but all changes will be in mathematical relation to time code.

When a sequence is referencing to time code, it's not necessary to start at the beginning of the song to be in sync with previously recorded tracks of the sequence. The sequencer calculates the measure and beat of the sequence in relation to the start time of the song. The tape can be started at any point of the song, and as soon as it receives time code the sequencer will find its place and join in, perfectly in sync. This is a great advantage over sync pulse (where the song must start at the beginning each time to be in sync with previously recorded tracks).

Most SMPTE time code is generated at the rate of 30 frames per second. This is the standard time code rate for audio machine synchronizing and for syncing to black-and-white video.

Sync to color video uses a different type of frame rate called *drop frame*. Drop frame time code is generated at 30 frames per second, but one frame is omitted every two minutes, except for minutes 00, 10, 20, 30, 40, and 50. Try not to think too hard about this concept—it will only confuse you! The reason for leaving these frames out is to make SMPTE time match the real time of color video. Color video operates at the speed of 29.97 frames per second, slightly slower than the 30 frames per second of SMPTE. Leaving these selected frames out

SMPTE Time Code Frame Rates

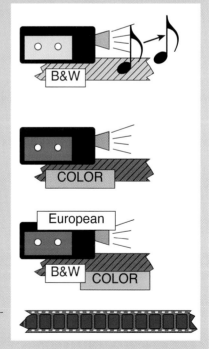

- **30 Frames per Second** – This is the rate for American black-and-white video and most audio-to-audio synchronization.

- **30 Frames per Second Drop Frame** – This is the rate for American color video to audio synchronizing. One hundred eight frames per hour are omitted to compensate for the National Television Standards Committee (NTSC) frame rate of 29.97 frames per second.

- **25 Frames per Second** – This is the rate for European black-and-white and color video synchronizing, established by the European Broadcasting Union (EBU).

- **24 Frames per Second** – This is the standard synchronization rate for film.

lets the SMPTE rate stay at 30 frames per second while maintaining real-time integrity.

The European standard time code rate, established by the European Broadcast Union (EBU), is 25 frames per second for color and black-and-white video. Film synchronization utilizes 24 frames per second.

MIDI Time Code

MIDI Time Code (MTC) is simply the MIDI equivalent of SMPTE time code. MTC uses real-time reference, like SMPTE, of hours, minutes, seconds, and frames per second. SMPTE time code, printed to tape, is read by a SMPTE reader and converted to MTC for time code communication within the MIDI domain.

Using Time Code

With modern digital equipment, you might never need to actually print SMPTE to a track, then connect that track output to a synchronizer that will cause the recorder transport to follow the time code positions. However, this is still a commonly used procedure in the studio, where analog and digital equipment are used together. Hence, you should be familiar with the basic functions and capabilities of an integrated system where SMPTE time code controls devices in your setup.

This is how the procedure for using time code works on most systems: There will be a sync out jack from your clock source, sequencer or drum machine. Sometimes sync out is labeled SMPTE Out, Time Code Out, or on some units, the sync pulse comes out of the Tape Out jack. Plug this jack into the line input of your tape recorder or the line input of the mixer, and assign the code to one of the tape tracks.

It's most common to record time code onto an outer track, also called an *edge track*. Usually the track with the highest number is designated as the time code track. On an eight-track, time code is typically recorded on track 8.

The suggested recording level for recording time code is usually between -9 and -3 VU. Time code doesn't have a very appealing sound, and the hotter the code signal is on tape, the higher the chance of it bleeding into the rest of the mix.

Sync pulse comes out of the sync jacks while the sequence or drum pattern is playing, so record a reference track of your drums while you record the sync pulse to an edge track. Later you can refine the drum parts as much as you want.

SMPTE time code, unlike sync pulse, can be laid down independently from the sequence. Usually, it's best to record continuous time code on the edge track of the entire reel of tape for the sake of convenience as you record more songs on the reel. Recording time code on tape is called *striping*.

Once the code is recorded on the tape, plug the output of the time code track into the device's sync in jack. Sync in can also be labeled SMPTE In, Time Code In or, on some units, the Tape In jack is used to accept time code.

When time code is successfully plugged into the sequencer, set the device to External Clock. This may also be labeled External Sync, Slave to External Sync, Slave, or just External.

If you're using sync pulse, simply play the tape. As soon as the sync pulses begin, the sequencer will start.

If you're using SMPTE, before you play the tape you must set the start point for the sequence in hours, minutes, seconds, and frames (02:05:37:02). Once the start point is defined within the sequencer, play the tape. The first beat of the first measure will begin at the start point you selected. From this point on, the sequence should follow along. Again, the advantage to SMPTE is that wherever you begin during the song, the sequencer will calculate the measure and beat, then lock into sync. The disadvantage to sync pulse is that you need to start at the beginning of the sequence every time to stay in sync with parts that are already on tape.

Being literate with time code is very important when it comes to optimizing the recording process. Everything we've seen so far about time code is used very extensively on many recording projects. You're capable of getting much more from your equipment if you're comfortable with synchronizing techniques.

Uses for System Synchronization

With the advent of powerful digital audio/MIDI sequencing software packages, it could be a long time before you need to synchronize digital devices. If you have a huge hard drive and you record only within your computer domain, you probably haven't needed to worry too much about synchronizing concerns yet. If you simply bounce your mixes to disk, then save them to CD or DVD, you're probably still immune to the sync plague. But if you need to record your mixes to DAT, if you're jumping into the digital mixer world, if you want to get the most out of your outboard digital effects, if you ever plan to interconnect to the professional world, or if you think your music has any chance whatsoever to make it to the next level of industry greatness, you're going to need to address synchronization in a serious way.

The power and flexibility of interconnecting the computer-based recorder with other digital devices is amazing.

MIDI to Audio Sync

MIDI to audio sync has made great strides in the area of convenience. Compared to manual sync, pilot tone, sync pulse, song position pointer, and FSK, the SMPTE-based system (often referred to as LTC (Longitudinal Time Code)) is fast, accurate, and fairly simple to master. SMPTE/MTC offers compatibility across the industry and serves us well in many cases.

Timing Discrepancies

MTC and SMPTE are good standards, but they're definitely not precisely accurate. The SMPTE to MTC translation is slow. It's dependent on the integrity and quality of the time SMPTE code. It often has to interpret what it thinks the time code should have been, and it's not always right.

Devices syncing to SMPTE/MTC float back and forth in time depending on a several factors:

+ Is the data transfer to and from the MIDI device going through a bottleneck, or can it flow freely and uninhibited?

+ Is the device's processor fast enough to keep up with the demand of the MIDI sequence data?

+ Is there digital audio data competing for the internal clock or computer processor power?

+ Is the MIDI interface keeping up with the demand for multichannel data transfer?

+ Is the master MIDI device running from its internal clock, or is it chasing another SMPTE-based device?

♦ Is there a grand master system clock acting as the time base for the complete system? If so, what kind of timing clock is it?

Many recordists feel that the SMPTE/MTC synchronization system is a perfect synchronization environment. It's not. The best accuracy factor we can hope for whenever using a SMPTE/MTC-based master is plus or minus a quarter frame. That might not seem unreasonable at first glance, but if we calculate the delay, we soon recognize a significant sync variance. If we assume a frame rate of 30 frames per second, it's easy to calculate that; because each frame occupies 1/30 of the 1000 ms in a single second, a single frame is about 33 1/3 ms. Each quarter frame is about 8 1/3 ms. A variance of plus or minus a quarter provides a net error of up to 16 2/3 ms, and that's touted to be about as good as it gets.

This degree of error is not too disturbing until you begin to combine devices, transfer data, and interconnect various systems over the course of time. With a plus or minus 8 1/3 ms error factor, the recordist can't be certain that every pass of every take in every generation will respond to synchronization in exactly the same manner. It's possible for the margin of error to compound over the course of a project, especially whenever you are combining recording formats and sync devices. The quarter-frame error factor can multiply throughout the life of a project, resulting in a musical feel that is much different from the one you slaved to create in the beginning.

Audio Example 8-1 demonstrates the rhythmic effect of the error factor in MTC and how it can compound over the life of a project.

Audio Example 8-1

Panned Clicks Simulating MTC Error Factor at 0, 8.333, 16.666, and 33.333 Delay

Audio Examples 8-2 through 8-4 demonstrate the sound of a drum track rushed and laid back by the potential margin of error in the MTC-based system.

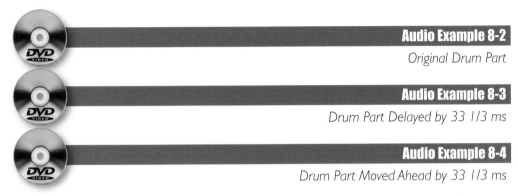

Audio Example 8-2

Original Drum Part

Audio Example 8-3

Drum Part Delayed by 33 1/3 ms

Audio Example 8-4

Drum Part Moved Ahead by 33 1/3 ms

There is no solution to this lack of accuracy as long as the master clock device is SMPTE/MTC-based.

MIDI to MIDI Sync

MIDI to MIDI synchronization is a reasonably simple process. MIDI Time Code (MTC) is simply transmitted through the MIDI cable connecting the synchronized device. Modern MIDI devices include an option to sync to an external source. Once that option is selected, the device waits to receive MTC, then plays along in near-perfect time.

MTC is a very common time communication format. Many digital devices and recorders synchronize according to MTC language. From previous study, we know that MTC is the MIDI equivalent of SMPTE time code, referenced to hours, minutes, seconds, frames, and sub-frames.

Accuracy

The accuracy factor of MTC in the MIDI to MIDI communication domain is much more solid than SMPTE-based audio to MIDI sync. An accuracy factor of plus or minus one tick can be expected in most

MTC Connections

Most software packages provide a way to send MTC and other synchronizing information to any machine or MIDI device in the system. Simply drag from one device to another to connect them through the digital on-screen patching system. Virtual patching like this is common in the digital domain.

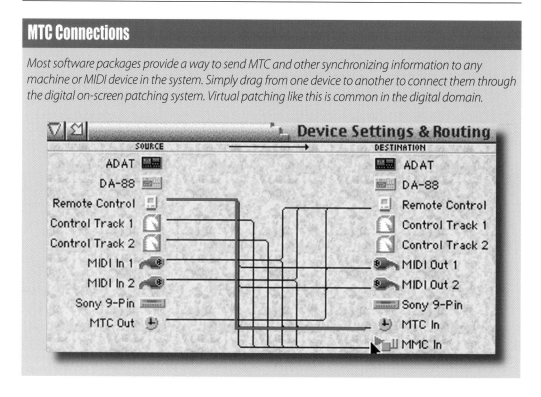

cases. (A tick is typically 1/480 of a beat.) Therefore, the accuracy is dependent on the tempo of the song. At 120 quarter notes per minute, we can expect accuracy to within plus or minus 1.04 ms (500 ms/beat÷480 ticks).

Accuracy in MIDI to MIDI sync (MTC to MTC) is still dependent on the same type of factors noted in the previous section: data bottlenecks, processor speed, time clock source, etc.

Logjam

If a MIDI transmission contains a lot of controller motion, such as pitch bend or modulation, the bulk of data can cause a MIDI logjam. Because all the data flows at once, sometimes it gets stuck, causing what sounds like a timing hiccup. The short pause, as the data regains its flow, renders the particular playback useless.

The logjam can be eliminated in a couple different ways. First, consider purchasing an interface with a higher data transfer rate. This solution can save you a lot of heartache later. Second, look for an option that lets you thin the controller data. This command might be called Thin Continuous Data, Thin Controller Data, or some similar, rendition. This command eliminates a percentage of the data. If you set the command to 50 percent, it will remove every other controller command, dramatically decreasing the bulk of the data. Most of the time, thinning data has no real effect on the sound of the performance, and it usually eliminates the MIDI logjam.

Processor Speed

Processor speed is very important, especially when using a digital combined audio/MIDI sequencing software package. It's likely that a large file with a substantial amount of digital audio will occupy the processor to such an extent that the timing clock bogs down. With this, the tempo and time feel go up in smoke. The solution to this type of problem is to either buy a faster, bigger, meaner computer; thin out your files so there aren't any unnecessary competitors lurking in the wings; or turn all nonessential system extensions off.

Analog-to-Analog Synchronization

Analog-to-analog synchronization typically involves reel-to-reel recorders. In fact, most of these analog principles apply to synchronizing digital reel-to-reel recorders, though there are other considerations we'll cover later that are unique to digital synchronization. In dealing with reel-to-reel machines, there still has to be a master and a slave device.

In this type of system, each machine has SMPTE striped on one track, providing a means for the synchronizer controller to evaluate the time address position of each member of the synchronization network.

LTC on Each Machine

Modern reel-to-reel recorders allow for external control of their playback, fast forward, and rewind motors. Typically, the motors are controlled by variations in voltage. The sync processor keeps track of the SMPTE (also called *LTC* or *longitudinal time code*) on each machine. It adjusts the speed of each motor so all transports run together with the master so that their SMPTE clocks are running along at identical addresses.

Therefore, with this system, there's a constant assessment of the individual slave speeds and LTC addresses. This continued assessment of position and adjustment of transport motors causes a phase shift effect between the synchronizing machines. There isn't usually a problem with this phenomenon unless there's identical material on two or more machines. If there is identical data, the resulting sound of simultaneous playback is a very pronounced phase shifting.

A system where a slave machine chases and synchronizes to a master machine is called a *chase-locking synchronizer*.

Verifying Sync

In fact, one way to verify the degree of sync between machines is to record identical material on each, then play both machines and listen to the identical material. As the machines run closer together, the phase shift gets tighter and tighter, but it never gets completely synchronized to the point where the resulting sound is smooth and wobble-free.

Offsets

It's typical that all devices in the synchronizing network run referenced to the identical address throughout the reel. If each reel starts at 01:00:00:00 and they always run together, everything makes more sense throughout the project and things seem to run smoother. If, however, you have multiple reels that all were striped with different starting addresses, you'll need to quickly master the offset.

An offset is simply a calculation of the difference in time address between the reels. If reel 1 starts at 01:00:00:00, but reel 2 starts at 01:00:45:00, there is a 45-second offset for reel 2. On the synchronizer controller, simply enter an offset of +00:00:45:00 for machine 2. The synchronizer will calculate the difference in time addresses throughout the reel, keeping the two reels locked together in relative sync.

Sometimes, in a system where sync has drifted over the course of a project, it might be necessary to search for perfect sync. It's usually with the offset control that you'll slide the machines into a tighter sync relationship.

Whenever possible, record a track with a very sharp percussive sound, like a clavé, onto a track of each machine while they're being simultaneously striped. This percussive sound will act as sync verification down the road if things start to go awry. After the reels have been striped, I like to run a sequencer, generating the percussive click, in sync with both multitracks while recording the click to both. This way, if the sync starts to sound out of sync later in the process, I can solo the clicks on each device and easily hear if sync has been maintained or lost somewhere.

Try panning the two clicks hard left and right. If sync is still okay the clicks might sound a little phased, but they'll seem to come from the center. The tighter the sync, the more centered the click will sound.

If the clicks are out of sync, it could be because one of the devices is being overworked and just can't keep a steady pace. It's also possible that somewhere along the line, the MTC/SMPTE margin of error exceeded acceptable boundaries, or it could be that corrupt code was recorded in the early stages of the project. For whatever reason it happened—and it does happen—bad sync needs to be addressed.

If devices aren't properly synchronized, the offset control can help slide them closer together. If you recorded percussive sounds on each device when they were verifiably sync-locked, play them back soloed and panned apart. Adjust the offset of the slave reel by sub-frames until the clicks move to the center and the phase shift is tight and clean.

Regenerating Time Code

Whenever copying from one tape or recording medium to another, regenerate any time code that's being transferred. Part of the problem in translating SMPTE to MTC lies in the inability of tape to accurately capture the SMPTE square wave. If the SMPTE wave wasn't

Offsets

Offsets provide a means to adjust timing between machines. If you come across two reels of tape or devices that must be synchronized, the time code references on each might not exactly match the other. In this case, the proper difference between the two time code positions must be guessed, then finely adjusted until the devices or machines work together in an efficient and musical way.

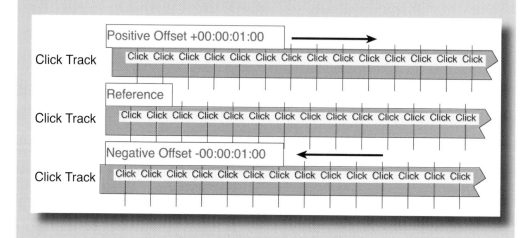

recorded accurately to start with, rerecording it from tape to tape only compounds the problem.

Regenerating time code is a simple process. Almost any time code generator outputs identical code to what it receives at its input. So, simply plug the output of the tape into the input of the time code generator. Then, patch the output of the code generator to the input of the machine being copied to.

Code that's been regenerated is as good as new time code. Most generators can even compensate for any time code dropouts that might have developed on the original track.

Regenerating Time Code

Time code that comes from a tape track often loses its precise definition in the recording process. Sometimes bits of code will be lost or damaged. Therefore, it's advisable to regenerate time code any time it must be recorded from one tape track to another. It's a good idea to regenerate the code even when it's coming from a tape track into a computer-based system.

The generator simultaneously outputs the exact code it receives at its input. In fact, it compensates for minor dropouts in the incoming code that might have been caused by tape anomalies or wear.

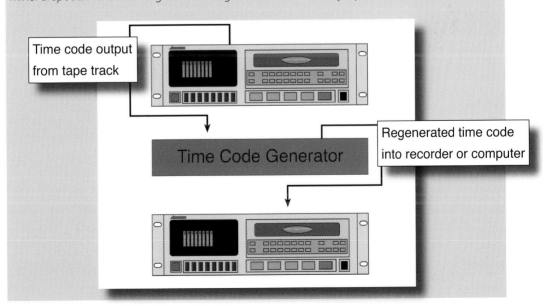

Time code output from tape track

Time Code Generator

Regenerated time code into recorder or computer

Freewheeling

Most sync controllers offer the ability to freewheel. Whenever there's a dropout in the flow of time code, the sync controller naturally wants to assume that the machine with the dropout has gone offline. In the harsh world of absolutes, a time code dropout causes the machine to stop. Then, when it sees code again, the controller chases and re-locks to the master. If this happens often in the middle of concentrated creativity, it's very irritating and displeasing to the masses.

The freewheel option lets the user determine how many frames can drop out before the controller assumes the machine is offline. During the dropouts, when instructed properly, the controller continues playback of the machine at the same rate as before the dropout. If the code comes back before the prescribed number of missing frames is up, nobody knows the difference. The machine keeps playing like nothing ever happened.

If the freewheel dropout boundary is set too high, the machines will take an unnaturally long time to stop once the stop button has been pressed. There's usually a good middle ground for this setting that minimizes undue stopping because of dropouts, yet keeps the session pace going by stopping relatively quickly after stop is pressed.

Jam Sync

Occasionally, the end of a song just comes too soon. If the time code stops near the end, you might be in a bind. If you've already got the early portion of the song sequenced, recorded, and synchronized, it's not practical to start over with new code.

This problem can be easily overcome through jam sync. *Jam sync* is like infinite freewheel. It follows the original LTC, regenerating fresh time code that can be printed on another track. Once the LTC runs out, the generator keeps generating code, even when it loses the reference code. If you keep the machine in record on the new code track, the generator will keep generating as long as you desire. With the newly generated fresh time code track, you can complete your recording and add any additional music you'd like.

Digital-to-Digital Sync

Digital-to-digital sync is similar to regular analog or reel-to-reel sync in many ways. There's a master and a slave machine, or several slave machines. The machines follow a time base reference and can chase SMPTE, LTC, VITC, MTC, and most other types of sync codes.

Though it's similar to LTC sync, digital sync offers a much tighter and absolute synchronizing scheme. Digital-to-digital synchronizing is typically capable of sample accurate sync.

Sample accurate sync has no drift and no phasing. It is as accurate as if the two recorders were one. The digital sync device analyzes sync at the sample level, maintaining a perfect lock at all times. This is a very cool feature!

Components of Digital Sync

Digital synchronization operates through the continuous control of three parameters:

- Time base
- Address
- Transport control

Time Base—Word Clock

Any time digital transfers are made, both the source and the record machines must reference the same clock. *Word clock*, which is simply the flow of data at the speed of the sample rate, acts as the timing constant between a source and a record deck. If the record deck isn't referencing the word clock of the source deck, the digital data can't transfer accurately—each sample is not seen completely, or maybe two are seen at once. Word clock must provide a stable, accurate measure of time passage.

When a record deck is set to external sync, it receives each sample in order from the source deck at its rate. Therefore, each word is transmitted accurately and in a timely manner. The two machines remain locked together sample by sample.

The concept of word clock isn't too different from the concepts of the earlier pilot tone and sync pulse. In each system, word clock, pilot

Sample-to-Sample Synchronization

Sample-to-sample sync provides absolute synchronization between multiple devices. This type of system contains a master clock that runs all digital devices; every time a sample is played back on one device, a sample is played back on all devices. It's important, therefore, that each device contains material recorded at the same sample rate. For example, a device containing audio recorded at 44.1 kHz will play back fast and higher-pitched when locked to a master device playing back at 48 kHz. Each sample in waveform B waits to play back until receives the go-ahead from the sample playback clock driving waveform A. The generator simultaneously outputs the exact code it receives at its input. In fact, it compensates for minor dropouts in the incoming code, which might have been caused by tape anomalies or wear.

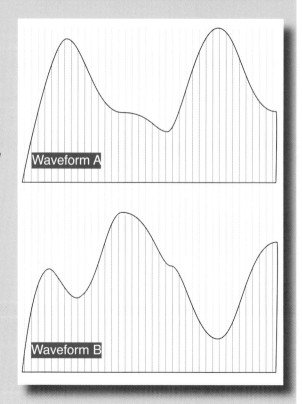

tone, and sync pulse, the slave deck moves ahead at the same rate as the pulse, cycle, or sample of the source device.

Word clock can synchronize through any digital communications/ transmission route, including S/P DIF, AES/EBU, SDIF-2, DA-88, ADAT, or a proprietary control track. Devices that require word clock communication for proper sync are digital mixers, stand-alone hard-disk recorders, computer-based digital audio workstations, and computer-based audio cards.

When devices are not referencing the same clock source during a digital-to-digital recording, the audio typically contains unwanted clicks, pitch wavers, and pops. These occur because of an abnormally high error rate due to data confusion as the data send gets out of sync with the data receipt.

Word Clock Rate

The word clock rate equates to the sample rate. The standard audio CD rate of 44.1 kHz is typically used for digital audio recordings that need to be released on CD. Although higher sample rates yield higher fidelity, the negative effects of sample rate conversion offset the benefit. Digital recordings destined to be mixed down to analog or through analog processing are best recorded at the highest available sample rate. Therefore, word clock time base reference could also be 48 kHz, 96 kHz, or even 192 kHz.

Pull-Up/Pull-Down

Pull-up and pull-down affect the sample rate, either by increasing or decreasing it by 0.1 percent. Therefore, a 44.1-kHz sample rate pulled down actually progresses at only 44055.9 Hz; if it's pulled up the sample rate becomes 44144.1 Hz.

NTSC video runs at 29.97 frames per second. Notice that 29.97 fps is 0.1 percent less 30 fps. There is a correlation between these two relationships.

There is a timing difference at each transfer stage when film is transferred to video for post-production and then transferred back to film again. Film runs at 24 fps. In the transfer process from film to video, every 24 film frames are mapped onto 30 video frames. However, the video then plays back at 29.97 fps. Since playback is 0.1 percent slower than the original transfer speed, any audio that's synchronized to the work video must be pulled down in speed by 0.1 percent. When the audio is transferred back to film, it will again play from the video at 30 fps. Since the audio was recorded at the proportionately slow speed, it will transfer in perfect sync to the film image.

If you're working on a film that's been transferred to video, select a pull-down rate on your sync controller. This will help ensure sync throughout the end of the film project.

Address Code

Word clock acts to synchronize the sample rates between two digital devices. However, in order to run together in relative sync and at exactly the right time musically, there must be an address code. The address code can take on several forms in digital communication.

MTC, SMPTE, VITC, Sony 9-pin, ADAT, DA-88, and Proprietary Control Track all have address information built in. Keep in mind that digital sync allows for combinations of time base and address code. As long as you're using a time hub that can read and write all of these forms of sync and time code, it only matters that there are cross-compatible time base and address masters at all times.

Transport Control

Whether using a hardware- or software-based transport, digital sync performs and feels like analog sync to LTC or VITC. The master controller calls the shots and the slave machines chase to a location, then they follow in perfect sync. All playback, fast forward, rewind, stop, and cueing functions are mirrored by the slave machines.

MIDI Machine Control (MMC)

MIDI Machine Control uses specific MIDI commands for controlling transport and cueing functions. Most modern recorders like those made by Alesis, Tascam, Sony, Fostex, Otari, and so on can be controlled through MMC. These machines must be connected, through standard MIDI cables and an interface, to the MIDI controller. The specific controller could be a software-based sequencing/digital audio package, a dedicated hardware controller, or a master tape machine.

Whether hardware- or software-based, MMC controls look and act like tape-deck-style transport controls. In a typical setup, the MMC controller sends transport commands to another MMC device which serves as an address master. The address master generates and distributes time code information to all recording and playback devices, which in turn chase and lock according to the MMC commands. It's not necessary that post-address master devices and machines respond to MMC commands; they must simply follow the timing commands supplied by the address master.

Variations in Accuracy

Not all devices support the same degree of synchronization accuracy. You might have purchased a device promising sample accurate sync. Then, when you connected it to your system, the sync seemed somewhat loose. That's probably because your system's sync is being controlled by the lowest common denominator. Devices that claim sample-accurate sync provide it only when connected to other devices specifically capable of sample-accurate sync.

There are four basic type of synchronization. Each type has a completely different degree of timing accuracy.

Sample-Accurate Sync

When devices run together in sample-accurate sync, they progress together on the sample level. They play sample 1 together, then proceed to sample number 2, then 3, then 4, and so on. Therefore, at a sample rate of 48 kHz, the devices track together at each of the 48,000 samples; this continues throughout the recording. This continuous tracking together results in the best possible synchronization.

The process of tracking together sample by sample also describes word clock. Sample-accurate sync, however, also keeps track of each sample throughout the recording. If the master machine starts at sample 1, all devices start at the very beginning of the recording. If the master device starts at sample 35,000,001, all devices go to that specific address and begin playing perfectly together. Ideally, no machine will be out of sync with the others, and that sync will be maintained without variation or phasing throughout the duration of the playback or recording.

A slight bit of *skewing*, or deviation from absolute tracking, might occur due to analog filter delays. But the delay will be very slight and absolutely consistent, so no phasing or adverse effect should arise.

Frame-Accurate Sync with Phase Lock

The term *phase lock* refers to the process described above, where the slave device tracks together with the master sample by sample. When phase lock is achieved, there is no drift between the devices. Frame-accurate sync, however, is bound to the accuracy of LTC/SMPTE time code.

Most systems using SMPTE and MTC are capable of phase lock, but their fundamental limitation resides within the quarter-frame accuracy factor of the SMPTE to MTC relationship. Although phase-locked, devices in this system cannot be trusted for sync accuracy closer than plus or minus a quarter frame. The net accuracy from take to take is therefore plus or minus a half frame.

The difference between sample-accurate and frame-accurate sync is only in the accuracy of the start point for playback—it will only be within plus or minus a quarter frame. But once the devices are synchronized, they'll stay as tightly synchronized, sample to sample, as sample-accurate sync. Considering the timing intricacies of an excellent musical feel, an error factor of plus or minus a quarter frame is disappointing and frustrating, though it's practically functional.

Frame-Accurate Sync with No Phase Lock/Continuous Sync

The accuracy factor for this type of sync within one frame is about a thirtieth of a second—plus or minus 33 ms. The variance factor of frame-accurate sync with no phase lock is substantial and continually changing. Since there's no link to word clock locking devices together once they achieve their relative sync status, the device transports are continually accessing sync status. As they assess their relation to the other devices, the only way to maintain sync is to speed up and slow down. An analog device continually varies the transport motor speed to maintain sync. A digital device must continually adjust the playback sample rate to keep pace. This is often called *continuous sync*.

The continual speed change as the transports adjust to maintain sync causes a pronounced phase-shifting effect between any two machines. A chorus-like sound occurs whenever identical material is being played back from different machines. Though it's not normal to play identical material from two sources at the same time, it's disturbing that the subtleties of the combined musical groove are continually varying. This is especially true considering that when a musical ingredient shifts within a pattern, sequence, or groove by a few milliseconds, the emotion and feel change dramatically.

Frame-Accurate Trigger Sync

Frame-accurate trigger sync has none of the continuous tracking or updating characteristics of the previous sync forms. *Trigger sync* is a very simple process; the master device tells the digital slave to start playing a specific sample at a specified frame. The slave plays the audio at its own pace, totally independent of any other timing source. Any audio more than a few seconds long is prone to drift out of sync, and there's no way to keep it in sync within this format. Trigger sync was used by early versions of most of the digital editing packages. It's a fairly useless system for anything other than triggering very short audio regions to play within one frame of where they really should end up. Frame-accurate trigger sync is archaic by modern standards.

Various Sync Formats

There are several different types of synchronization formats and schemes. One ingredient of a complete synchronizing system doesn't ordinarily make a complete package. Time base, address code, and transport controls are fundamental to a rock-solid synchronization setup.

Internal

The internal sync clock for any digital device is pretty solid and consistent. Some devices can even play back over long periods of time, staying fairly close together with no synchronization other than a precisely timed press of both start buttons. However, internal sync is primarily for playback and recording within a one-device closed system.

Some devices have a relatively inaccurate and inconsistent internal timing clock. If a device like this can be controlled by word clock or another very accurate external sync source, it's usually worth the effort. An inconsistent timing clock can have an adverse effect on audio quality. Synchronizing to a more reliable time base reference will result in higher-quality digital audio.

MTC

MIDI time code is not a bad choice for synchronizing a MIDI sequencer to another MIDI-sequencing device. The resolution of accuracy is plus or minus one sequencer clock unit (often called a *tick*). It's common for computer-based sequencers to divide each beat into 480 ticks. However, when synchronizing digital audio devices, MIDI time code provides the least amount of time-base stability. Using MTC as a master source for time base and time code is inadvisable. Even if MIDI Machine Control is required for system completion, you'll get much better results if you use a more accurate time base and address source.

SMPTE (LTC)

SMPTE (*Longitudinal time code*, or *LTC*) is commonly used as a time base in the analog multitrack domain. One track of the multitrack—typically the track with the highest number—is striped with SMPTE. SMPTE time code provides the address information for a synchronizing system. When used in conjunction with MTC and MMC, timing resolution and accuracy aren't exceptional. As stated earlier, the accuracy within plus or minus a quarter frame can have an adverse effect on the musical feel.

LTC-to-LTC synchronizing systems are fairly accurate within the analog multitrack domain. The sync controller typically keeps the machines within a subframe of each other. This accuracy is dependent on the integrity of the time code and the ability of the transport mechanism to maintain sub-frame accurate sync. Although LTC-to-LTC sync is relatively accurate, the slave transport still continually varies its speed while searching for perfect sync.

Video Sync

Video sync, also called *house sync* and *blackburst*, is a constant timing reference used in situations where multiple video tape recorders, switchers, edit controllers, and audio devices must interconnect accurately and reliably. The clock frequency of house sync is exactly 15,734.2657 Hz.

Without a timing constant like house sync, video devices do not interconnect well; they'll produce image glitches, rolling pictures, and other time-related inconsistencies. House sync serves to ensure that the leading edge of each video frame and time code address happens at the exact same time, therefore continuously controlling the accuracy and stability of the system.

Audio devices also benefit from house sync. Although it doesn't increase the initial accuracy of a time address system, resolving all audio devices to this constant time source helps them lock together accurately. Once relative sync is achieved, all devices run smoothly together without drift because each transport tracks the crystal-generated blackburst.

VITC

Vertical Interval Time Code (*VITC*, pronounced *VITT-see*) encodes the same SMPTE address and code structure information as LTC into the video signal itself. With VITC, there's no separate LTC track. The time code information resides in a portion of the video signal, called the *vertical blanking interval*, that's outside the visible video image.

Since the time code information is part of the video signal, a professional VTR can accurately read it at all speeds: fast, slow, and still framed. A VITC system provides for quick and accurate placement of audio segments and sound effects in relation to the video image.

Normal work-copy video, called a *window dub*, contains an actual scrolling image of the exact time code reference throughout the video. VITC systems are accurate enough to eliminate the need for such a dub.

Word 1x

Word 1x is standard word clock. It serves as the master time base for most digital audio systems. Systems that resolve word clock maintain rock-solid sync, free from inter-machine phasing and drift. Using word clock as a time base doesn't by itself ensure sample-accurate sync. But it does ensure that once sync has been achieved within the address code limitations, it will remain stable and constant.

Word 256x

Word 256x, also called *super clock*, is used by Digidesign hard-disk systems as their time base. Like Word 1x, this time base reference serves as a guide clock.

S/P DIF and AES/EBU

S/P DIF and AES/EBU are similar to word clock in that they act as the stable time base in a digital recording setup. These sync protocols specify one device as the master and one as the slave. The slave tracks the master, typically in phase lock—the digital data flow is perfectly in sync—though there's no address code information. S/P DIF and AES/EBU synchronization protocols do, however, have provisions for embedded time address information, though it's not typically implemented.

S/P DIF and AES/EBU are different from word clock in that they contain digital data as well as time base.

SDIF-2 and MADI

SDIF-2 and MADI are digital connecting systems that separate the word clock time base reference from the digital audio data. Word clock reference is typically connected through a separate BNC connector.

Proprietary Sync Systems

Several proprietary sync formats are in common use. Manufacturers develop synchronization schemes that they feel offer prime support for their specific product needs. Alesis, Tascam, Mark of the Unicorn, Digidesign, and others have sample-accurate sync systems for their equipment. Although these platforms are proprietary in their development, other manufactures occasionally support or borrow them in their product designs.

ADAT and DA-88 Sync

These proprietary sync systems are very stable and precise. Sample-accurate sync information, including time base and address code information, is transmitted in the data stream along with the audio information. Complete sample-accurate sync is achieved between ADATs or DA-88s through direct unit-to-unit communication. Only in the older ADATs is an external control required to attain sync.

ADAT and DA-88 sync is so precise and rock-solid that sync ports can be daisy-chained with no loss. Standard configuration limits on complete systems are capable of utilizing up to 16 units chained together for 128 tracks.

Index

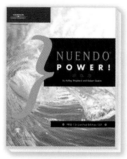

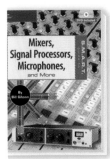
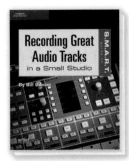

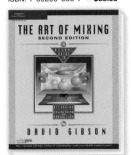